Exploring Visual Design

Exploring

Joseph A. Gatto

Los Angeles Public Schools

Albert W. Porter

*California State University
Fullerton, California*

Jack Selleck

Los Angeles Public Schools

Visual Design

Consultants

Gerald F. Brommer

George F. Horn

Davis Publications, Inc.

Worcester, Massachusetts

Gene Gill worked with line on several levels in this work. Black lines were painted on an aluminum surface and red lines were applied to a clear acrylic sheet that was placed over the aluminum. The lines seem to come alive as the viewer walks past the work, which is 37¼″ x 37¼″.

Copyright 1978
Davis Publications, Inc.
Worcester, Massachusetts, U.S.A.

Printed in the United States of America
Library of Congress Catalog Card Number: 78-55398
ISBN: 0-87192-101-4

Printing: Kingsport Press
Binding: Kingsport Press
Type: Malibu by W. A. Krueger Co.
Graphic Design: Penny Darras-Maxwell

10 9 8 7 6 5 4 3 2 1

Contents

Before Beginning

For the next few months you are going to be looking inside art. You are going to see what makes it work and how it is put together. You will learn why some of the things that are put together look better than others, and why some works of art please us more than others do.

In effect, you will be looking at the structure of art, because that is what *design* is. And in order to learn about design you will be looking at its *elements* (its parts and how they work), and its *principles* (the ideas and guides that show us how to use the elements).

You will be working with the same visual vocabulary that artists have used since ancient times. You will see what others have done with some ideas that have proved their effectiveness over many years by experimenting with these ideas and becoming aware of the rich visual resources around you. You will learn how to apply what you have learned to your own work.

The authors of this book have flooded you with words and pictures, ideas and concepts, projects and problems—more than you can possibly use in one semester or even a year. We want you to be selective. Pick out projects that interest you, projects that will benefit you the most. We have supplied a wide range of information and projects to help each of you grow in your understanding of design. We hope we have included just the right ones for you.

One of the first and most basic things you will learn about design is that its elements and principles work together. And although we will concentrate on each element and principle separately, no one of them ever appears in a work alone. When you study line, for example, you will also read about how it relates to shape and form, or space and texture, or rhythm and movement. Soon you too will be able to talk about how the different elements and principles interact with one another.

Because this is true, you will notice something about the illustrations in the book. Each is meant to explain some idea in the text that goes with it. But even though every picture has a reason for being where it is, it could just as easily be somewhere else! In fact, if the work is well done and carefully designed, there is no reason why it could not help show us every bit as much about shape and contrast as it could explain about balance and unity. Usually each picture caption will stress one major idea or clarify some statement made on the page that goes with it. But again, don't forget that all the elements and principles of design really do go together.

As you read this book and study the illustrations, take the time to go back to earlier chapters and compare statements and ideas. For example, see if what has been said about line will help you understand pattern better. Look for uses of texture and space in the works chosen to show you about contrast and value. Each chapter should fit with every other.

And when you finish this book, think about the countless examples of design all around you: in nature, in works of art, in your whole environment. You should be more aware of how design is a part of your life—both now and in the future.

Andrew Wyeth (*Ground Hog Day, 1959*) and Pierre Bonnard (*The Breakfast Room*, c. 1930–1931) have painted similar subjects, and both artists have shown the same concern in their paintings for the qualities of light, value, shape, and space. Yet each work is unique and highly personal. The principles of design never dictate the finished work; they simply guide and point out directions to take. *Ground Hog Day, 1959* from the Philadelphia Museum of Art. *The Breakfast Room*, oil on canvas, 62⅞ x 44⅞″. Collection, The Museum of Modern Art, New York.

This striking architectural design shows the interior of Frank Lloyd Wright's Guggenheim Museum. There is movement in its curves, balance in its rings and open spaces, and unity in its cylindrical structure. Courtesy of The Solomon R. Guggenheim Museum, New York.

What Is Design?

This is a book about design and how its principles and elements affect our lives and the ways we look at and make art. When we say, "That's a great design," we are showing just how broad this word's meaning can be. We may be talking about a fine drawing, a challenging painting, a startling piece of sculpture, an exciting piece of jewelry, an inspiring new building, or an interesting layout for a housing development. In all these examples we are recognizing a sense of *visual order*—many different parts brought together to make a unified whole.

Design has narrower meanings. Simply putting things together, organizing the parts of a work, can be designing. Even simpler is the art of decorating. Applying a decal to a notebook or T-shirt, just adding a covering to something, is a way of designing. For years, designing cars meant changing strips of chrome, making longer or shorter fenders, and rearranging tail lights. But this should really be called *styling*, because it doesn't show the sense of purpose, the idea of total unity, that design shows.

Design involves thinking about the *purpose* for a product or work of art. What effect do we mean to have with what we make? Who will see it or use it? What is its *function*? And what are the relationships of the different parts to the whole? The more we think about these kinds of questions, the better our designs will be.

How do we know when a design is good? One of the best ways we can learn how to judge the quality of things is by *training* our eyes to see expression and purpose in the objects and forms that make up our world. If we don't exercise our senses when we drive by a building, open a package, read the cover of a book, or buy a piece of furniture, we'll never experience the excitement and pleasure this active looking can bring—both in the works of other artists, planners, and designers, and in the things we make ourselves.

Design in Nature and the Human Environment

When you think about it, design—good, bad and sometimes just indifferent—is everywhere. There are more opportunities for training our judgment, stimulating our visual curiosity, and adapting creative ideas for our personal use than we could ever exhaust.

The Elements

Nature, with its almost unlimited supply of forms, is a great source of design. It has always been a primary stimulus for artists, and it may well be the best place for you to begin your study and application of the elements and principles of design. Especially helpful is the way nature offers so many diverse forms and combinations. Think, for example, of what nature can do with the single design element of *line:* the thin, curved stems of waving flowers; the parallel, running ridges of sand dunes; the intricate lineal markings of tropical fish. We can easily see that line isn't just one type of mark or edge of a form. Line can be thick or thin, straight or curved, angular or rounded, ragged or smooth.

And we can say the same kind of thing about all the other elements of design: *shape, form, color, value, texture,* and *space.* Together with line, these six elements are the basic parts of any design. They are the fundamental tools of the artists and designer. They are the first simple vocabulary of the person who wants to say something visually. These elements are rarely, if ever, seen in isolation; both nature and artisans always combine them.

Did you ever try to design something using only lines? If you did, what happened when you suddenly decided that one line should circle back on itself or cross another line? The word *circle* should be enough of a clue. You found yourself forming different *shapes.* In the same way, many different lines together can create the feeling of *texture,* and if they are bunched closely enough, they can produce an area of dark *value.* Study architectural drawings done in perspective. Do the converging lines, lines running together at some fixed point, make you see and feel the depth of *space?*

The possible combinations of design elements are almost endless. There are colored shapes and textured shapes. These shapes can create shadows of varying values, and when the values change, the sense of space changes with them. Texture can enrich form, and form can carve out space. This kind of relationship simply goes on and on.

The Media

Almost as important as the elements and principles of design are the *media.* These are the materials that an artist or craftsperson chooses to help express his or her ideas. An architect knows that a certain kind of shape, marked by lines so as to produce a certain texture, will look one way on paper and quite another way in granite or marble. Just imagine how differently you might feel about your own school, for instance, if everything about it stayed exactly the same except that its natural bricks suddenly became painted cinder blocks or pre-cast concrete! Even the shade of red you were used to would never look the same on such different surfaces, no matter how closely you tried to match it.

Every medium has its own special qualities. Whether you want a feeling of warmth from the colors you are painting with, or a look of smooth perfection in the facade of the building you are designing, you will always have to think about the media you are working in. Certain pigments, inks, papers, drawing instruments, and raw materials produce certain effects, for both the beginning student and the skilled professional artist.

The Principles

There are no iron-clad rules for putting together the various elements of design, but there are *principles*— general guidelines and sensible directions that have worked for a long time for many people. These principles are: *balance, unity, contrast, pattern, emphasis, movement,* and *rhythm.* They can be studied, modified, juggled, and used to help you create. Best of all, they work equally well in all media and in all artistic activities, from painting on canvas to planning a city park. Once you have experienced and learned these principles, you will be able to see them everywhere and reproduce them in your own work.

Like the elements, there are infinite examples of the principles of design in both nature and our human environment. Also, like the elements, the principles are never found in isolation. Whether in a painting, sculpture, or building, they must work together

Line, shape, and value are elements of design that exist in nature and in Karel Appel's *Dragon Over the Village* (1953); but could nature ever express exactly the feelings and ideas of the artist in this picture? Courtesy of the Martha Jackson Gallery, New York.

Max Bill's sculpture has been carved and polished to produce a smooth form with open spaces and dark shadows. Notice how the values of the granite still give this work a feeling of rough and varied texture.

Many short lines produce a pattern on the sides of this fish. But notice the contrasting values of its head with the rest of its body, the forms of its fins and gills, the way its sides appear to have a rougher texture than the other parts of it because of its lineal markings, and the way a sense of space seems to radiate from the center of its body.

with the elements for maximum visual effect. Balance, for example, one of the most important principles of design, may involve opposing the form of an extended arm to the form of a contracted leg in the sculpture of a human figure. Or, it may mean dividing different kinds of colors in different areas of the plane of a picture. These are ways of balancing design *elements*. But balance could also mean moving light and dark values against one another to achieve contrast or emphasis, which are design *principles*.

Looking, Learning, and Judging

Remember that you will never know whether a design is good or bad, strong or weak, uplifting or depressing, engaging or just distracting, unless you take the time to look at and think about design in your world and the work of others. To gain this knowledge and be able to draw on a solid background, you should start by examining the works of experienced professional artists and designers. Be selective, but stay curious! Every exciting graphic design that gives directions in a large store, every newly created environment in your city, every fashion show, printing and typography display, architectural fair, manufacturing and packaging exhibit, or automobile show represents the ideas of some artist or designer working to achieve excellence.

Another way to improve your design sense and judgment is to stop and take another look at the thousands of objects that are part of your daily life. You may not have realized it, but every time you wear one piece of clothing rather than another, decorate your wall with one poster instead of another, or prefer a particular car, painting, or piece of furniture to another, you are judging the elements and principles of design.

Just as design has influenced your past through the great works of civilization, and your present through the countless objects, products, and forms of your daily life, it will surely be a part of your future. In the years ahead designers will be concerned with your entire environment. All the spaces that surround you, the total quality of your life, every part of your world, from the smallest package to the largest city, will represent a challenge to their skills and yours, whether as a designer or a judge of design.

That is one of the reasons why this book offers so many examples, illustrations, and suggested activities—to help train your eye, build your knowledge, and improve your skills and judgment.

The Start of an Answer

This chapter began by asking, "What is design?" By now you should be able to answer that question in some general but fairly important terms, by talking about the *elements, media,* and *principles* of a work. The artist or craftsperson visualizes the elements in certain media, arranges them according to certain principles, and arrives at a thoughful, unified whole. The rest of this book is devoted to providing more detailed answers—to helping you see, recognize, and understand the elements and principles of design in the art of others, and to showing you how to apply these same elements and principles to your own efforts at visual communication.

Le Corbusier has designed this chapel as if it were a huge piece of sculpture, and the results are exciting. There are both interior and exterior worship spaces. Notice the strong contrast between the soaring lines of the sharp-edged roof and its feeling of massive weight. The tower is a tall vertical structure, but what principle of design makes it fit so well with the rest of the building?

The elements and principles of design that we study and use today are the same as those used by the painters, sculptors, printmakers, and artisans of centuries ago. Regardless of their media, the 17th-century Japanese printmaker, the 19th-century French painter Georges Seurat, and the contemporary American sculptor Chuck Arnoldi, have all had to deal with the problems of shape and value, rhythm and unity, and line and light. Japanese print from the collection of Joseph Gatto. Seurat painting *(Study for LeChahut)* courtesy of the Albright-Knox Art Gallery, Buffalo, New York. Arnoldi enamel and tree branch sculpture *(Stick-Up)* courtesy of the Los Angeles County Museum of Art.

Every art has its tools. Just as writers use the elements of language (such as nouns and verbs) as their tools for saying things, artists and designers use the elements of line, color, value, shape, form, space, and texture as their tools for expressing ideas visually. These tools are the means of making statements in graphics.

The elements of design are everywhere in your world. They help make that world fuller, more exciting, and more meaningful by appealing to your senses. For example, think of the lines you see every day. They can be two-dimensional, like the grid on a piece of graph paper, or three-dimensional, like the branches of a tree. Telephone wires are solid lines—lines in space. But those same wires in a drawing or photograph are flat. They are lines in a single plane. How would you describe the wrinkles in your hand, or the grooves and ridges in a rock?

Just as lines can have two dimensions or three, so can *shapes*. A *shape* is flat; when it is solid we call it a *form*. A circle is a shape, for example, but when it becomes a sphere it is a form. A triangle is a shape, but a pyramid is a form.

Shapes and forms don't have to be geometric figures, though. Every physical object you see has a form, and every picture of it has a shape. So these elements of design fill your world just as lines do.

This is true of all the elements. Just try to imagine your world without color! Or think of what that world would be like if all its colors were equally dark or light. *Value* is what we call this contrast in the intensity of light. It is a useful tool in design and an exciting part of our environment. By slowly changing the shading in a drawing of an object we can make it seem more or less solid, rounder or flatter. A building in bright sunlight and deep shadows is an impressive example of what *value* means.

The surfaces of all things have *texture*. Sponges, feathers, gravel, ice—every rough, smooth, hard, or soft material in our world feels different to the touch. By using line and value we can recreate the sense of these textures in our designs.

Eggs are solid spherical forms. But what would they look like in this two-dimensional photograph if the shadows disappeared? Values of light and dark can create the illusion of substance.

The use of space in a painting can make you feel many emotions. Andrew Wyeth calls this work *Christina's World* (1948). How large is that world to the isolated figure on the hill? Tempera on gesso panel, 32¼ x 47¾". Collection, The Museum of Modern Art, New York.

The rich, solid handle of this comb contrasts with its fine, long, straight teeth. What two basic elements of design are dominant in this work by Al Ching?

Part One:

The room you live in is a *space*. If it is a rectangular room, you may think of it as an empty box. But since a box is a *form*, one way of defining space is to think of it as *negative form*. If you hollow out a solid object, you have an enclosed area in three dimensions: an interior.

But don't stop there. Space can also mean the whole range of your vision when you're standing on the edge of the ocean. Or it can be the illusion of depth in a painting, or the total area of a billboard or movie screen.

Every artist and designer uses the elements of line, color, value, shape, form, space, and texture differently. Bold, slashing lines can show great force and energy, or fine, rhythmical lines can suggest peace and quiet. The basic tool of shape can express one thing when it is painted on canvas and something very different when it is etched in metal. A shape carved from marble may show a certain purpose or creative feeling on the part of the sculptor that cannot be duplicated when cast in bronze.

The greater painter Rembrandt used strong, contrasting values to give the figures and objects in his pictures a solid, powerful feeling of three-dimensional form. But some modern painters, like the minimalists, use such close values that you almost cannot see where one shape or color ends and another begins. There are practically no gradations.

Some artists, like Matisse, van Gogh, and Gauguin, use color as a dominant part of their painting. Others, like Franz Kline, barely use color at all. Some designers want rich surface qualities in their work, so they create heavy textures. Others may want to emphasize a different element of design; they use plain, smooth surfaces.

Today, designed spaces are getting bigger and bigger. In Colorado and California, the environmental artist Christo has hung great curtains of fabric in canyons and huge fences of cloth miles overland.

These are the elements of design. The more we know about them and the better we understand them, the more exciting our visual world becomes.

The Elements of Design

16

In an untitled silkscreen print (24″ x 24″), artist Gene Gill used line to create an exciting pattern of red ink on a white background.

Line

Much of what we know about early civilizations is recorded in line drawings, etchings, and paintings. A young child's first art expressions usually emphasize the use of line. We can find examples of line everywhere: in nature, architecture, clothing, food, artworks, and utilitarian objects. Have you ever walked along a dirt road or a sandy beach with a stick in your hand? It is almost impossible not to draw or leave a mark of some kind. Perhaps it is just a meandering line that follows you, or a particular line pattern or design done either subconsciously or by plan.

In art, we may think of *line* as the path made by a pencil, pen, crayon, or other drawing object. We may also consider line to be anything thin, or long, such as wire or string. A shape consisting of generally parallel edges that is decidedly longer than it is wide—a tall, thin tree, for example, is a linear shape.

Types of Lines

Following are definitions of some of the more commonly used types of line. These definitions may vary from place to place.

Outline

Generally, an outline refers to the outer edges of a shape or object—what would show if it were silhouetted against the light. Tracing around an object is one way to do an outline.

Contour

Contour lines also outline the shape or form, but they also include surface lines. For example, you would draw the outside edges of a figure, but you would also show surface lines—such as folds in clothing, and lines describing facial features. Usually, a contour line is done very slowly, with concentration on subtle changes in line direction. In doing a contour drawing, try not to remove your drawing tool from the paper or to look at the paper. This exercise, called *blind contour drawing*, will develop eye and hand coordination. With more practice, you will be able to vary the thicknesses of lines to suggest form and shadow.

This "imaginary wire" drawing was done with pencil. Emphasis was placed on capturing the sense of action and movement—*not* on correct proportions.

Gesture (Movement)

Gesture lines are quick lines that emphasize direction and movement. An interesting way to use this technique is to imagine that a thin, continuous flow of wire is coming out of the drawing tool. Also, you must quickly describe the figure by looping, twisting, and changing direction with the imaginary wire. Many believe that drawing contour lines and drawing gesture lines are the most valuable exercises to help gain movement, confidence, and knowledge in your work.

Blocking-in

Blocking-in lines are quick lines that emphasize angles and directions. Perhaps most important, they divide your picture into areas so that the arrangement of the parts (composition) is pretty well determined before you begin more detailed, finished work.

Sketching

Sketch lines suggest shape, texture, and value. Sketches can be done very quickly, barely suggesting the subject, almost like notations. They can also have a more finished appearance. Sketches emphasize information gathering. They are often preliminary drawings for more finished works to be done later, perhaps with different materials.

Calligraphy

Calligraphy comes from Greek words meaning "beautiful writing." In your art class, the study and practice of beautiful handwriting could be one objective in itself. Often, however, the purpose of studying calligraphy is to gain an appreciation for the beauty of the line forms and to carry this awareness into other areas of art.

Line as Direction

As we communicate with handwriting, most of us read or write lines. Individual letters and words are made up of lines that are straight, curved, and looped in directions that have meaning for us. The artist also uses line to show direction. The quick lines behind a cartoon figure help show that the character is moving fast in a certain direction. In a more complicated work, lines may lead us to certain areas in the design or help establish the structure of the artwork.

Line has direction. It pulls our eye up a tall tree or "jiggles" it as we drive by a picket fence. The basic

Artist James Fuller used many kinds of lines in his pencil drawing, *Wayne with a Bird* (1966). Attention is brought to the face, where darker, more concentrated lines are used to describe the shading, hair, and features. The bird is represented by lighter, more delicate lines, and the whole picture is unified with a sharp contour line.

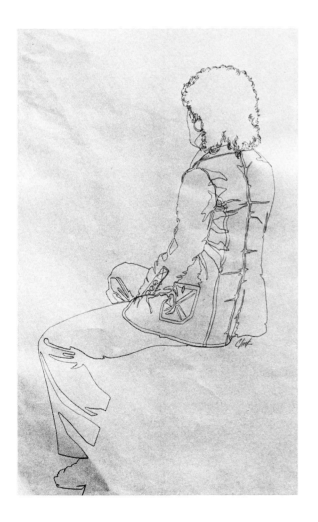

A high school student did this fine contour drawing. Note the changes in the direction and thickness of the line.

lines—vertical, horizontal, curved, and diagonal—
have some general characteristics, or "personalities,"
that can aid the artist in his or her purpose.

Vertical lines remind us of ourselves standing. They
also bring other associations to mind: skyscrapers, sol-
diers at attention—stability, dignity, tallness. Horizontal lines may suggest the ocean, the horizon, the
body at rest—calmness, repose, breadth, quiet. Diagonal lines suggest falling, leaning, and growing—
lines of action, movement, tension, drama. Curving
lines have a sense of sweeping, turning, and bending—the edge of a cumulus cloud, the rings of a tree
trunk, the curling smoke from a chimney, or the fast
curves of a roller coaster.

Line Personality

The quality of a line can reach our emotions and suggest mood. Nervous, quick strokes can add a sense of
tension or drama to a drawing or painting; a firm,
smooth line may give us assurance and allow us to
view it calmly. Fuzzy, blurred lines may suggest a
dreamy, mysterious mood, while repeated curving
lines alternating from thick to thin might achieve a
hypnotic effect.

Line Variation

Artists can take us on line journeys, perhaps through
the use of a flowing, curving, looping line done with
brush and ink or through the fluorescent tubes used
in neon art. An artist can use geometric shapes, with
their sharp edges and sudden directional changes, to
produce a feeling quite different from a flowing line
design.

Yet another artist may use short, quick, ungraceful,
scratchy strokes. Our journey becomes filled with de-
tours, stop signs, and yield signs as we work our way
through the design.

The artist's purpose and/or mood will determine
the kind of line she or he wants to use. The artist may
wish to represent some objects as they actually appear, and he will describe them with accurate outlines, shading line strokes, and varied line thicknesses. A cartoonist, on the other hand, may want a
sense of believability in cartoon characters. He or she

Lines follow the forms of the individual objects in this etching and capture the different textures and patterns. Some
lines are very delicate, as in the wings of the flying insect.
Other lines are short, crisp, and bold, as in the background
mountains. What other line variations do you see? James
Fuller, *Dappled Things Series*, #44, 1976, aquatint-mezzotint
(17″ x 22″).

Lyonel Feininger used the woodcut medium and angular lines to express the extreme action of a sailing ship in a severe storm. Collection of the Norton Simon Museum of Art at Pasadena.

Heavy lines were used by a Japanese printmaker to create the image of a fish, which has been printed on fabric.

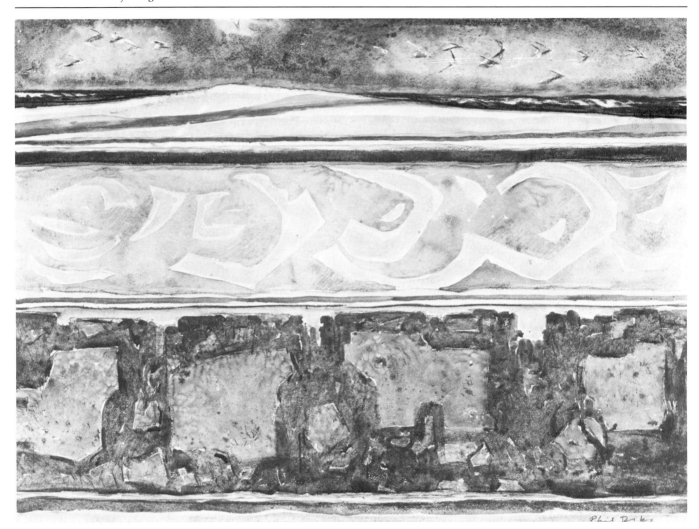

Horizontal lines and bands were used by Phil Dike to capture the quietness and orderliness of a coastal setting. Rocks, water, and sky were stylized to fit the artist's composition. *Sea Structure #15* is 22″ x 30″.

may use a simpler outline style with a few well-placed lines that suggest movement or expression. Another artist may use non-objective lines (lines that represent no recognizable objects). A variety of such lines may suggest action or mood, or they might just provide visual enjoyment.

Line Structure

Structure is the "bones" that hold materials, things, or ideas together and make them weak or strong. Structural lines can be delicate and thin like a spider's web, or thick and bold like the pylons supporting a pier. A bridge may be safe or collapse because of its structure or lack of it; likewise, a painting might look "well put together" or might visually "fall apart" because of its structure. Sometimes strong and delicate lines are used together in interesting and exciting combinations.

Vertical and Horizontal Lines

Lines that are straight up and down (vertical) or straight across (horizontal) suggest strength and both physical and visual balance. Piet Mondrian was one artist who created strong designs with vertical and horizontal lines. His work seems very simple, but much effort was spent in putting each line in exactly the right place. Often, this took many hours of arranging, moving and rearranging. The strength and simplicity of his work has been an inspiration in many areas of modern art—architecture, clothing, and furniture, to name just a few.

Although an artist may use only vertical and horizontal lines, they can lend considerable structural variety. Where lines cross or touch, different sizes of rectangles will result. The length of the lines can vary. The different shapes inside the lines can create a sense of space, movement, and visual balance.

You might try a "Mondrian-like" design. Use some black tape or strips of paper on a piece of illustration board or heavy paper. Allow a few lines to run off the top, bottom, and sides. Then start to attach some lines of varied length, keeping them vertical and horizontal. Determine what begins to happen visually concerning balance, space, and movement. Do parts of your design look too heavy? Too weak?

Photograph by Britt Phillips.

Piet Mondrian, *Composition in Red, White and Yellow*, 1938. Los Angeles County Museum of Art. Mr. and Mrs. William Preston Harrison Collection.

Angled (Diagonal) Lines

Because angled lines suggest movement, they can have a dramatic and dynamic appearance. When combined with horizontal and vertical lines, the same effects can be achieved. The strength of angled lines can be seen in the geodesic form created by Buckminster Fuller. The series of repeated triangles is used in many structures, from playground climbing units to modern architecture. The triangle has great strength, both actual and visual.

The interlocking triangles that describe the structure of this playground climbing unit are based on the geodesic form created by Buckminster Fuller. In a more complicated structure, the triangular motif is also used in the third dimension.

Many areas around school provide line structure subject matter for the observant art student. This solitary figure was photographed on a stairway.

Powerful brush strokes, some running off the canvas, create
a dynamic structure of bold lines and shapes. The viewer
can almost "feel" the artist's brush movements. Franz Kline,
The Ballantine, 1948–1960, oil on canvas (72″ x 72″). Los Angeles County Museum of Art, Estate of David E. Bright.

Curved Lines

Curved lines may also be part of structure. An example is the curving forms of a mammal's rib cage. Another would be the curving line of a wagon wheel with the straight spokes radiating from the central hub. Curving lines allow the artist to change direction, bend a shape, or present a nucleus from which other lines and shapes can visually move.

Select an interesting but common object like the protractor, as Frank Stella did (opposite), or perhaps something from the classroom or your home. Repeat the shape with thick and thin lines. Interweave them and break up the lines and shapes. Choose a few simple colors and complete the design.

Structure lines can be delicate, fuzzy, or blurred and still be visually balanced and structurally sound. Certainly the spider's web is delicate and beautifully woven and, for its purpose, well constructed.

Blurred lines or lines of varying darkness change a design's sense of space. The similar thick lines in the Mondrian design keep the forms from shifting visually in space. To illustrate how delicate, blurred, softened, and varied lines change a design, do a variation of the Mondrian design by making some of these changes. The blurred lines will seem farther away, the bolder lines will advance visually, and the overall variety of lines should completely change the sense of space and structure. Both pictures will have structure, but of a different nature.

A wealth of line structure can be found in our surroundings—playgrounds, factories, stairways, windows, trees, telephone poles, boats. Be aware. Take mental notes, take photos, or make sketches that you can use as motivation for your own artwork.

Circular lines and colors overlap each other, and might symbolize overlapping water rings or sound waves. Courtesy of BirthdayBook, Ltd., New York.

This large painting uses the wide lines of the protractor shape interweaving in the center, while thinner lines separate shapes and colors in the central area. If you look closely, you'll see that the artist varies the basically symmetrical design and keeps the structure from possibly becoming boring visually. Frank Stella, *Protractor Variation*, 1969, fluorescent-alkyd on canvas (20' x 10'). Los Angeles County Museum of Art.

Prehistoric deer. Courtesy of Natural History Museum of Los Angeles County.

In this fine painting by Stuart Davis (1894–1964), lines are implied where shapes and colors come together. *Premiere,* 1957, oil on canvas (58″ x 50″). Los Angeles County Museum of Art.

Compare this to the Davis painting.

Implied Lines

Lines can be implied where they do not actually exist. A row of tall trees can suggest a line that leads your eye into the distance. Your eyes will also fill in the space between a series of dots or marks, thereby creating a line. Edges of objects, shapes, or forms, flying sparks in a factory, or the repeated water flow of a fountain also imply line. You might like a new car because of its *lines,* or you might be impressed by the *lines* of a building. In other words, the contour shapes suggest line.

Large forms may appear as lines when viewed from a distance: a freight train rolling across the landscape, members of a marching band, or freeways or rivers viewed from the air. Some artists even create large earthworks (linear excavations in open desert areas) that are best viewed from high in the air.

Line is also implied in a design where two shapes or areas of color come together. A change of texture or pattern in touching shapes, whether in a drawing, a painting, or a sculpture, may still give a sense of line even though the edges of the shapes are not sharply defined.

Often, implied lines are produced when you work with shapes or colors, and are not planned. You should be aware of their existence and potential and begin to use them intentionally. Removing the color areas and lettering from the Stuart Davis painting leaves only the edge lines, thereby illustrating the importance of implied lines.

Like a series of tunnels connecting small craters, the sun-dried cracks in the earth lead to the hoof prints of a horse. To gain the effect of viewing large forms that become lines when seen from high above, imagine that you are thousands of feet up in the air looking down—the cracks and hoof prints might then be rivers, canyons, and so on. Photograph by Ann Plauzoles.

Thousands of light bulbs create many lines as our eye connects the individual lights and completes their linear movement.

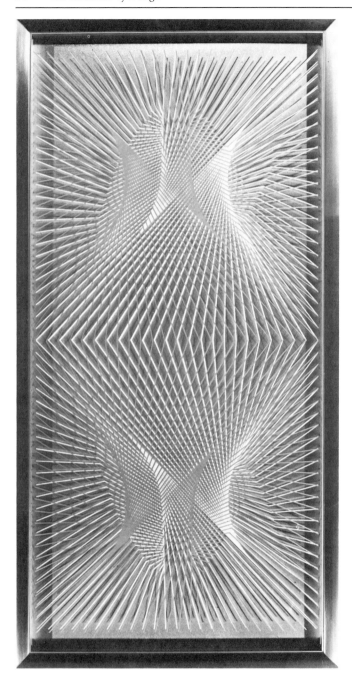

Linear arrangements are painted in silver and white on aluminum and clear plastic in an untitled work (37¼" x 19¼") by Gene Gill. Great complexity can be achieved using only lines that are carefully measured and painted.

Line as Texture and Pattern

Texture is an object or shape's surface quality—whether it is, for example, rough, smooth, or fuzzy. Pattern is the repetition of an element—often shapes that are determined by *lines.* Texture and pattern are discussed more fully in Chapters 6 and 11. Here, we will discuss how you can see and use *line* on surfaces to create texture and pattern.

Some texture and pattern can actually be experienced by touching, such as a plaster carving. Quite often, however, the artist must use techniques that merely suggest texture and pattern.

Experiment with different tools and techniques to discover ways of using line, texture, and pattern. Draw with twigs and ink or with an eraser into a charcoal surface, perhaps overlapping lines until a texture and/or pattern develops.

You also might try carving into a plaster block with tools that create a pattern with lines of varying thicknesses. Perhaps you could base your idea on something in nature where texture and pattern are prominent: the rough bark of a tree, the stripes on an animal, the veins on a leaf, or the etched patterns and textures on a canyon wall. You might create recognizable forms or simply use their suggested lines as a starting point.

Other things you see may give you ideas for texture and pattern designs using various materials. Ordinary things such as chairs lined up at an antique store may be springboards for pen and ink designs or stick constructions. You may not wish merely to copy what you see, but to use the information to develop your own ideas. For example, the chairs at the antique store might inspire a line design based on their vertical lines contrasted with bolder horizontal and slightly curved lines. The result might have no recognizable reference to the chairs.

It is easy to overdo texture and pattern. When working on a design, ask yourself if the texture of pattern you're considering has a real purpose. Will it add a *needed* visual interest? Will the pattern be boring or will you include other ideas to balance the visual power of pattern? Would the design be more effective if you omit or tone down the line texture or pattern?

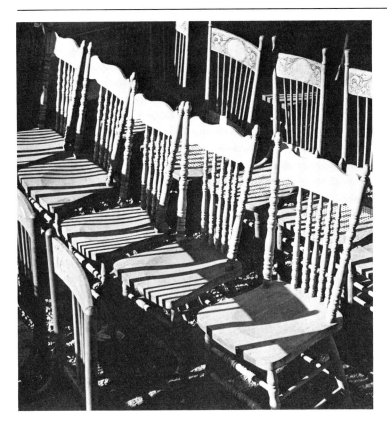

Try the exercise mentioned in the text that refers to this photo. Can you do a design inspired by this photo with no recognizable objects in it?

Carved lines simply illustrate the arms in this sculpture called "The Kiss" (1912) by Constantin Brancusi. The comparatively smooth texture of the bodies is balanced by the carved line texture of the hair. Philadelphia Museum of Art, Louise and Walter Arensberg Collection.

Broken, jagged lines might evoke a sense of apprehension, irritability, or concern.

Being aware of how lines can suggest moods will help you both view artwork with more understanding as well as convey meaning more effectively in your own creations. For example, if you want to capture the sense of speed and beauty of a running animal, you would want to choose certain materials and techniques, perhaps strong, flexible wire or a flowing line of ink or damp paper rather than heavy pieces of wood.

Line combinations can be seen everywhere. A telephone pole can be seen as a heavy, bold line, with thick and thin lines (wires) attached to it. The trunk of a tree may have thick, textured lines, while the branches are thinner lines, the twigs still thinner, and the veins in the leaves thinner yet.

An artist uses line combinations for specific reasons. To draw a coat representationally (that is, as it actually appears), you might use a heavy, curved line for the shadowed edges of the coat and thin, delicate lines for the edges that are in strong light. You might use sharper, angled lines to represent the folds in the material, and curving, smooth lines for the general shape. Perhaps short, quick, *criss-crossing* strokes (cross-hatched) would suggest the texture of the fabric.

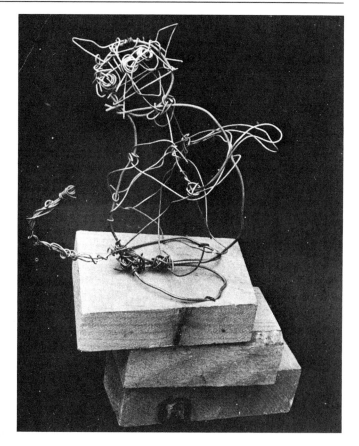

The three works of art shown are created from very different materials: an oil painting by Joan Miró, a wire sculpture animal by a high school artist, and a woodcut by Karl Schmidt-Rottluff. All use line variety in different and exciting ways. In Miró's painting, *Animated Forms,* he uses very thin, flowing, moving lines contrasted by the two bold, thick lines (shapes) in the central area. The three layered shapes at the bottom center act as a springboard for the other lines to visually bounce from and lead our eye up and down and through the design (see color photo on page 33). The wire cat combines looped, twisted, angled, and curved lines to form a comical and expressive animal form. Schmidt-Rotluff's woodcut is very dramatic for many reasons. First, he cut into the wood with bold, angled strokes and mainly straight lines that quickly describe each shape—*across* the nose, *down* the cheek, *back* to the head. Compare these bold, angled, straight lines with the curved lines in the cat or the floating forms in the Miró. How did the different materials chosen by the artists affect their designs?

Joan Miró, *Formes Animées*, 1935, oil on canvas (76½″ x 68″). Los Angeles County Museum of Art, Estate of David E. Bright.

Karl Schmidt-Rottluff, *Christ and Judas,* woodcut (19″ x 17″). Los Angeles County Museum of Art.

A junior high school artist made various-sized loops from reed and carefully placed different colored pieces of cellophane inside each one. The curving lined shapes seem capable of helping the small figure in the balsa wood chair to fly away.

Lorser Feitelson, *Hardedge Line Painting*, 1963, enamel on canvas (60″ x 72″). Los Angeles County Museum of Art.

Other Design Projects

Take a piece of blank paper that is about 6 inches x 24 inches. Place it vertically on your desk, an easel, or on the floor. Think about starting a design on it. Imagine yourself sketching or painting the design. Then turn the paper horizontally and do the same thing. What differences occurred in your imaginative design? Did the shape of the paper influence your thoughts? How?

Try a small non-objective drawing, using *only* vertical lines. Then do the same type of drawing using only horizontal lines. You might even turn your vertical drawing sideways when you're done to make it horizontal. Do you see and sense a difference in the drawing's mood or character?

From what you know about curved lines, you may want to try a curving line design using basket reed for a three-dimensional project, or even try tagboard strips that can be glued by their edges to a flat surface.

Using a brush and ink or paint, try to produce as many different kinds of lines as possible without making any recognizable images. Thick, thin, straight, curved, fast, slow. What are their different characteristics? Can you describe them in terms of personality?

Depending on your drawing ability and interests, draw the same thing (a still life, a human figure) using a slow contour line; a fast, sketchy line; and bold, thick lines. Compare the three drawings and discuss their similarities and differences.

Do a wire sculpture of an animal or human form emphasizing movement and action by exaggerating the form. Find examples of artwork or photos where the artist has used this technique.

Listen to various kinds of music. Without making recognizable things, see if you can capture the rhythm and feel of the music, using only variations of lines.

Bring fruit, vegetables, or other natural objects (leaves, bark, flowers) to class. Cut through the fruit or vegetables to see the internal line structure and design. Base a design of your own on one of these objects. Add other lines to it if you desire.

The bentwood rocker is based on a design from the 1860s. The curved lines suggest calm movement and relaxation, as a rocker should. Let your finger follow the lines starting at the bottom of the rocker and move to the arms and up and across the back to sense the rhythmical design.

To help understand that lines are suggested by the edges of objects, use a piece of dark paper and an X-acto blade to cut away the negative shapes (shapes between objects such as the sky and ground, between and around the limbs and trunk of a tree, the background behind a figure or still life, and so forth). Then mount the dark paper on a light color with rubber cement.

Take your name or a favorite word and use five different drawing materials and five different line strokes for five separate name or word designs. Compare them. What differences exist?

Put a piece of tracing paper over a favorite photo, drawing, painting, or design. Taking care not to damage the picture below, look for and draw the simple lines that suggest the structure of the work. Remove the tracing paper and compare the simple structure lines with the artwork. This exercise may help you see how the artist organized the original picture.

Use a felt marker to draw five horizontal lines that are fairly closely spaced. Now add ten vertical lines, allowing some of them to go across the horizontal lines. Then begin to add diagonal and curved lines where you wish until the design appeals to you. Try to analyze why you put the diagonal and curved lines where you did and what effect they have on your design.

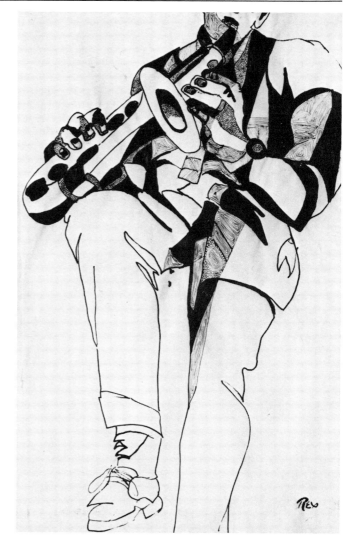

A contour drawing was done from a model and then the student artist darkened in some areas and shapes, using line and solid areas to create value contrasts.

Artist Gene Gill used carefully ruled pencil lines in this untitled drawing, which is 46 inches high.

The brighter the light source, the brighter the colors. Notice the dulling effect of shadows on the colors in the background.

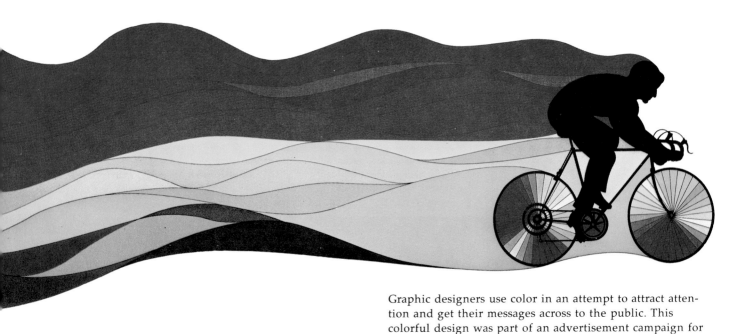

Graphic designers use color in an attempt to attract attention and get their messages across to the public. This colorful design was part of an advertisement campaign for a soft drink, and used all the spectrum colors as well as several tints and shades. Courtesy of 7-Up Company, St. Louis.

Color

Color is one of the most exciting aspects of our environment. It is an element of art that appeals directly to our emotions and is universal in appreciation. It creates an immediate impact on small children as well as adults, on artists as well as observers.

We see color that is sometimes bright, sometimes dull; exciting or bland; harmonious or chaotic. We cross streets filled with color, enter stores filled with color, and make purchases because of color. We know color affects our communication, because it designates and identifies the things around us. Also, by surrounding ourselves with color, we can establish moods. Some colors, such as school colors, cause us to cheer, shout, and scream. Other colors make us cry and feel unhappy.

Color constantly changes with the time of day or the amount and quality of natural or artificial light. There are probably many unique colors in your immediate area waiting to be discovered: rusted signs, neon lights, buildings, clothes, foods, the sky, plants, and many other everyday objects.

In short, color is vital and necessary part of our lives. It is important that we learn where color comes from, what its properties are, what it can do for the artist, and how it can be used, mixed, and enjoyed in the art you create and observe.

The Source of Color

Color differs from the other elements of design in that it deals with certain scientific facts and principles that are easy to understand. Color in artwork or the things we see is derived from light, either natural or artificial. Where there is little or no light, there is little or no color. Under a strong light, the color of an object is more intense.

The sensation of color is aroused in the human mind by the way our vision responds to the different wavelengths of light. If you allow white light (such as sunlight) to pass through a glass prism onto a piece of white paper, you will see that the rays of light are bent, or refracted. As they are spread on the paper, your eyes pick up various colors, caused by varying wavelengths. We call these individual bands of color the *spectrum:* violet, indigo, blue, green, yellow, orange, and red. You have seen this same grouping of colors in a rainbow, where the raindrops act as

40

COLOR WHEEL

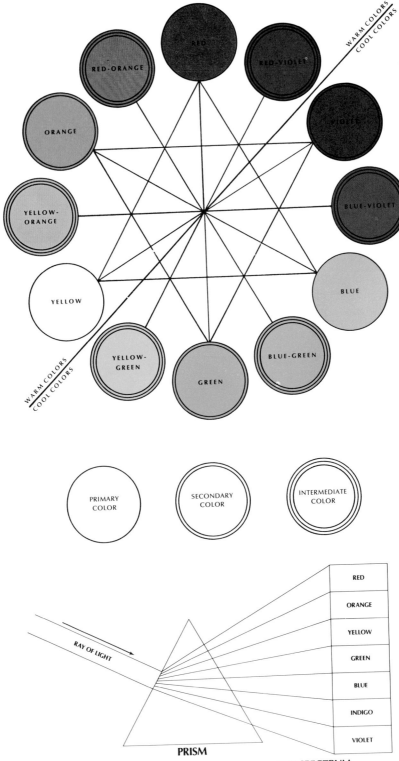

the prisms. For easier study, the spectrum can be arranged in a circle, called a *color wheel.*

When white light falls on a *red ball,* all the colors of the spectrum are hitting the ball. All wavelengths (colors) except red are absorbed into the surface of the ball, while the red ones are bounced off it. You call the ball red because when you were very young you learned that the visual sensation caused by the wavelengths is the color *red.* Each color and all the color mixtures that bounce back to your eyes are interpreted the same way.

The colors of the light spectrum are, of course, true color and represent the greatest intensity of brightness possible. The coloring matter that artists use are neither as intense nor as pure as spectrum colors. Artists' colors come from pigments, which are combined with other substances to make various paints, crayons, waxes, pencils, pastels, or plastics. Pigments are powdered substances (from nature or the chemical laboratory) that provide the color for art media. Physicists work with light itself, not the reflected light of pigments. (Although some artists now use electricity and light to create works of art which can be projected on a screen or glass.) Their mixing and use of colors is slightly different from those of the artist. You might find it interesting to compare how a physicist works with the spectra and light with how an artist uses pigments.

The Neutrals

Not all objects have colors found in the spectrum. Some are black, white, or gray. They merely differ in the amount of light that is reflected from them. Because we do not distinguish any one color in them, these tones are called *neutrals.*

White is the sum of all colors. If all the color waves reflect equal amounts of light, white is the result. A white surface reflects back to our eyes all the light rays shining on it, absorbing more of them. What we see is the color of the original source of light.

Black is the total absence of light. It results when a surface absorbs all the color rays and reflects none of them. Place a white swatch and a black swatch of material or paper in sunlight for several minutes, then feel the surfaces. The black swatch will be much warmer because it has absorbed all the light rays from the sun, while the white surface has reflected them all and absorbed none. Can this help you understand why it is popular to wear light-colored clothes in summer and black or dark colored clothes in winter? Or why peoples in warm climates paint their houses white?

Gray is created by only a partial reflection of all the color waves in the spectrum. The more light that is reflected, the lighter the gray; the more that is absorbed, the darker the gray.

All color waves reflected equally. None are absorbed at all.

All color waves reflected equally, but only partially. All are absorbed equally but partially.

No color waves are reflected at all. All are absorbed equally.

All possible colors can be made by mixing the three primary hues in various combinations of intensities. In this set of illustrations, you can see how the full-color printing process uses the three primary hues, plus black, to create all the colors of the original painting. When tiny dots of yellow and red are placed over each other, orange is formed. The closer the dots are placed together, the more intense the color. Perhaps you can look through a magnifying glass to see these tiny color dots.

To get the four steps shown here, the original painting is photographed four times. In each case, a filter is used to eliminate all reflected light except the hue being photographed. So a picture is taken of all the yellow hues; then all the red; then all the blue; and finally all the black. These negatives are etched onto metal plates, and inks of the same hues are used to reprint the images to paper.

This process mixes the three primary hues and the neutrals (for value contrast) to form an almost exact copy of the original painting. It is fascinating to notice how much of each hue is present in all areas of the painting, showing that the colors are made from a visual mixing of the three primary hues.

The Properties of Color

Three properties of color can be defined and measured: *hue, value,* and *intensity.* Sometimes these properties are called dimensions, qualities, or characteristics of color.

Hue

Hue is the name of the color itself. It refers to the color's position in the spectrum. The wavelength of blue, for example, is 19 millionths of an inch long, while the wavelength of red is 30 millionths of an inch long. Each hue has a definite wavelength and can be placed in its proper sequence in the spectrum.

Red, yellow, and blue are the three *primary hues,* sometimes called the elementary hues. All other hues can be made by mixing these three. (Notice their location in the color wheel diagram.)

A color may change its hue by being mixed with another color in the spectrum. Mixing colors actually changes their wavelengths. If you mix equal quantities of any two primary colors, you produce *secondary colors.* Red and blue will make violet; red and yellow will make orange; and blue and yellow will make green.

In addition, certain *intermediate* hues can be created by mixing a primary color and a neighboring secondary color. There is actually no limit to the number of intermediate hues possible. The proportion and amount of primary and secondary colors are the dictating factors. Refer again to the color wheel for a visualization of these mixtures.

Make a color chart by mixing your own colors, using tempera or watercolor paints. Starting only with the three primary hues, mix three secondary hues, and then six intermediate hues. Paint the colors on a design or on swatches that can be cut and pasted in place on a wheel design or chart. The resulting colors may not be exactly what you are expecting because the primary colors may not have been pure spectrum colors. If any of the primary colors is slightly off its required position in the spectrum, the resulting mixes will also be slightly off color.

An artist can check the values and value contrasts in a painting by squinting his or her eyes to shut out some of the light source. Another way to check values is to take a black-and-white photograph of the full colored painting. The print will show only the various values and not the colors. Both color contrast and value contrast are essential in most paintings, especially those that are representational. *St. Basil's, Moscow* is a watercolor by Gerald F. Brommer.

Value

Color's *value* distinguishes between the lightness and darkness of colors, or the quantity of light that a color reflects. There may be many value steps between the lightest and darkest appearance of any one color. Machines have been invented that can distinguish many millions of values, although our eyes can pick out relatively few.

If you think of light falling on a green ball, the part of the ball nearest the light will be lightest in value because it reflects the most light. The part that is opposite the light source will be in deep shadow, and thus it will be the darkest in value.

Adding white to a hue produces a *tint* which is a lighter version of the color. Pink, for example, is a tint of red that is made by adding white to red. Many tints of red are possible depending on the amount of white added.

Adding black to a hue produces a *shade.* Mixing red and black creates a dark value of red; the value depends on how much black is added.

When the neutrals (black and white) are added to a color, only the value is changed, not the hue. If you try to make colors darker by mixing a darker hue (such as deep blue or purple) to it, the value will change, but so will the hue.

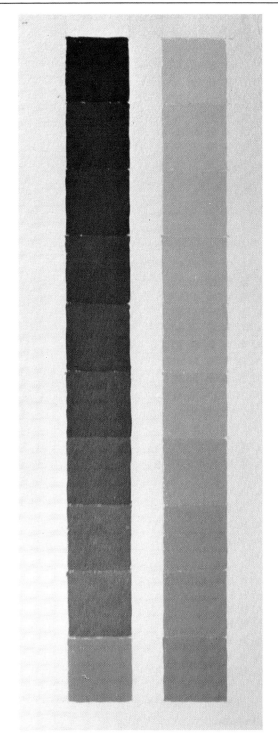

Notice the value differences that LeRoy Neiman uses in his painting *Hank Aaron.* Lighter values are in the background, and the contrast makes the figure stand out. Notice also the use of cool colors in shadows instead of black. Some intense colors (yellows) are lighter in value than other intense colors (red and blue).

The spectrum orange hue is at the bottom of each column. Black, in increasing amounts, was added to one column, and white to the other, to develop a range of shades and tints.

The colored yarns in the "God's eyes" are intense in their hues. In the direct sunlight they seem very bright. Notice the effect of shadow (lack of light) on the same hues in the background.

The hues in Helen Lundeberg's painting *Cloud Shadows* seem dull, grayed, or tints of the original hues of blue and green. The abstract shapes provide the impression of landscape without showing us any particular place. Courtesy of the artist, collection of Mr. and Mrs. Sidney Brody.

Intensity

The third property of color is *intensity,* which refers to the *quality* of light in a color. In this way, it differs from value, which refers to the *quantity* of light that a color reflects. We use the term *intensity* to distinguish a brighter tone of a color from a duller one of the same hue. For example, a color that has a high degree of saturation or strength is more intense than a color that has been grayed or neutralized.

There are actually four ways of changing intensity of colors when mixing pigments. We have already discussed two of them: adding white to produce tints and adding black to produce shades. As white is added to any hue, the resulting tone becomes lighter in value but also loses its brightness or intensity. In the same manner, when black is added to a hue, the intensity diminishes as the value darkens. Your investigations will show that you cannot change value without changing intensity, even though these two properties of color are not the same.

The third method of changing intensity is by adding a neutral gray, of the *same value,* to the spectrum color. The mixture then is a variation in intensity without a change in value. The color will become less bright as more gray is added, but it will not take on a lighter or darker value.

You can also change intensity by using color. When you work with the primary colors—red, yellow, and blue—the mixture of any two (for example, red and yellow) will make an intermediate hue (orange). The remaining primary color, blue, is known as the *complement* of orange because it completes the spectrum. Thus the fourth way of changing the intensity of any hue is by adding some of its complementary hue.

Try mixing two of the primary hues to make a secondary hue. Then add a small amount of this color to the remaining hue (its complementary color). Then add a small amount more again and again, until you have a wide range of intensities. By doing this, you are dulling the original hue and making it grayer by adding its complement. The hue is also changing because you are not adding the neutrals.

You will note that as you mix these complementary colors, bit by bit, a neutral gray will be formed. This is because the complementary colors represent an equal balance of the three primary hues. Theoretically, they should produce white. The pigments are not perfectly pure, however, so a gray is the result.

Intense colors cause a feeling of excitement in Robert E.
Wood's watercolor painting, *Flame at the Top.* Courtesy of
the artist.

Robert Patrick Rice has used the complementary hues of red
and green in his landscape painting *Shade.* Red is mixed in
varying amounts with green, and green is mixed in varying
amounts with red, to obtain a wide variety of grayed colors
that have less intensity than the original hues. Courtesy of
the artist.

You might also notice that in some combinations of complementaries, a range of brownish hues will be created. This occurs where there is more red and yellow in the mixture than blue. This information can be helpful later when you work on other art projects, or whenever browns are not available.

Color Harmonies

Perhaps you have discovered, or perhaps someone has told you, that certain colors "go well" together. Other colors may clash when placed side by side. Such determinations are based purely on individual likes and dislikes. One person may think that certain colors clash, while another may think they appear harmonious.

Designers and artists have worked for years with certain combinations called *color harmonies*. We know, for example, that complementary colors, opposite each other on the color wheel, provide maximum visual contrast of hue. If strips of these colors are placed next to each other, they tend to produce a vibrating sensation to our eyes. It is difficult to fix our eyes on the line where the two fully saturated colors meet. Op artists use this knowledge to create designs that seem to sizzle and vibrate.

Look at the color wheel and list all the complementary harmonies that are possible. You might like to make some design using equal amounts of one of these combinations, or make a chart that shows these harmonies. You can use each of the complementary combinations to produce grays and browns.

Analogous colors are those that have a single color in common and are next to each other on the color wheel. Because of this common color, they naturally relate well to each other. In fact, they are sometimes called related colors. Yellow-green, green, and blue-green are analogous colors. How many analogous harmonies can you get from the color wheel? It might be interesting to make a painting or design, using only analogous colors, perhaps adding black and white to make tints and shades.

Another three-color harmony is called *split complementary*. Begin at one part on the color wheel, say at blue. Go across the wheel to blue's complement, which is orange. Then take the colors that are analogous to orange: yellow-orange and red-orange.

Jasper Johns used a complementary color harmony (blue and orange) in his painting *Numbers in Color*, 1959 (66½" x 49½"). Collection of Albright-Knox Art Gallery, Buffalo, N.Y., gift of Seymour H. Knox.

Kwan Jung uses an analogous color harmony in his watercolor *Morning America*. The warm hues seem saturated with warm sunlight. Collection of Southern Utah City College.

A split complementary color harmony (blue-violet, yellow, and orange) is employed by Jan Hoowij in *Dual Focus*. The artist also grayed some hues outside the two circles and used neutrals to change values. Courtesy of the artist.

Color and image are joined in a powerful statement about contemporary civilization. Joseph Mugnaini, in this etching, *The Tower*, uses a triadic color harmony (red, blue, and yellow) of intense hues to communicate his message. Courtesy of the artist, collection of Joseph A. Gatto.

These two hues, plus blue, form a split complementary harmony. Because such combinations form sharp contrasts, they are often used in bright posters or paintings. With this particular combination, the major background parts of the poster might be in yellow-orange and red-orange, with the contrasting blue used for the center of interest or main message.

Still another three-color combination is *triadic harmony.* A triad of things means three things, so triadic harmony involves three equally spaced hues on the color wheel. Red, blue, and yellow are a triadic harmony, and so are blue-green, red-violet, and yellow-orange. Which other triadic harmonies can you find in the color wheel?

If you were a designer (interior, industrial, graphic, fashion, etc.) what use could you make of these color harmonies? Would you always use the hues at their full intensities? What could you mix with them to lessen their intensities?

Warm and Cool Colors

If you look at the color wheel again, you will see a line that divides it in half, separating the warm colors from the cool colors. These colors, however, are not measurable warm or cool. The range of hues from yellow to red-violet are called *warm colors* because we associate them with warm objects or circumstances. Can you think of things—fire, the sun, desert sand, for example—that are warm and are in the warm color range? The *cool colors* range from yellow-green to violet. Can you think of cool things that have these colors?

An artist painting an ocean subject might use cool colors to accentuate the icy feeling of the scene. Warm colors might help express heat in a painting of men working near a blast furnace. These examples are obvious, but artists and designers do use these characteristics of color to help communicate their feelings and ideas.

Our minds and eyes react in certain ways to these colors. Warm colors, especially reds and oranges, seem to come toward us in paintings, designs, or photographs. Cool colors, especially greens and blues, seem to recede, or go back. If you make a design where the major portion is in blues and greens and then place a spot of red-orange on it, the small area of warm color will appear to come forward from the surface. This phenomenon occurs because of the length of the light waves reflected from the surface and the way our mind interprets them. How can a designer or painter use this knowledge? If you wanted a small room to appear larger would you paint it with warm or cool colors?

Monochromatic Colors

If a painting is made by only using one color, plus black and white, it is called a *monochromatic* painting. Contrasts are achieved not through the use of color, but through the use of value changes. All the parts of a monochromatic design, room, painting, or drawing will work well together because only one hue is involved.

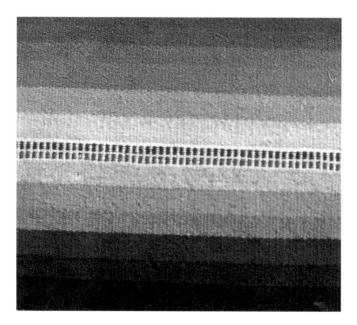

The Navajo Indian who wove this blanket contrasted warm and cool colors. Because the weaver lightened the values of the colors as they approached each other, the intense complementaries do not clash. The neutral spaces around the small squares of intense color also keep them from clashing.

Designers working with clear, stained glass must often use and balance both warm and cool colors to keep the window (and therefore the lighted interior) from feeling too warm or too cool.

Other Design Projects

Using compass and ruler, work out a unique circular design that can be colored with the hues of the spectrum. Use only the primary colors of tempera paint to produce all the colors. Or you may wish to use a full spectrum of crayons, watercolors, or colored pencils or markers.

Cut the spectrum hues from colored magazine pages. Trim and arrange an interesting design that will illustrate the circular arrangement of the spectrum hues.

Select a monochromatic magazine subject that has predominantly cool colors. Cut a warm color spot or subject from another illustration and paste it in a central location. Does the warm color seem to come forward?

Select a variety of colors from magazine sources and cut them into equal rectangular sizes. Arrange them in order so that some seem nearer and others seem farther away because of their warmth or coolness. Paste them on a neutral colored sheet. Can you do anything with the sizes of the swatches to enhance the feeling of distance and nearness?

From magazines, select and label monochromatic, analogous, complementary, and triadic color harmonies.

Set up a classroom still life composed of dominant cool colors with warm accents. Reverse the combination in another part of the room. Photograph them or paint them to accentuate these combinations.

Any color may vary in appearance, depending on the color adjacent to it. Select a color swatch from a magazine or use pigment to create a 2-inch by 2-inch sample of color. Place this color swatch in ten different color environments (solid color sheets, or patterned paper, or color photographs from magazines). Observe how color changes when seen against different environments.

Select the flags from various states or countries. After a bit of research, can you make statements about how color was used as symbolism?

Select five to ten words—such as virtue, honesty, evil, danger, cowardice, life, hope, death, happiness, joy, innocence, royalty, wealth. Find or create colors that symbolize these words. Perhaps you can letter the words with the colors, or create a colored illustration that shows these words in graphic form.

Warm and cool contrasts, together with complementary harmony (red and green) are used in a tissue paper collage. Because of the intense colors and contrasts, the pen-and-ink line should have been somewhat stronger, or else omitted.

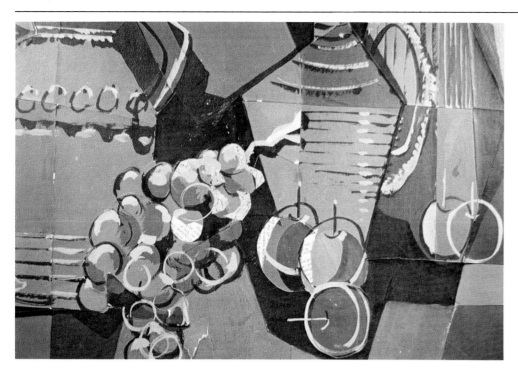

This is a detail of a collage and painting project that used only one color plus black and white. The yellow shapes were added for contrast in the center of interest area.

Value is the lightness or darkness of color. The fender and the body of the car are actually the same color, but because of varying amounts of light on them, they have different values, and parts are darker in value.

Value

All things around us are illuminated by some light source. Without light, we would not be able to see anything in our environment. No matter how bright you paint your walls or how colorful your brightest clothes are, you cannot see them in absolute darkness. With a little light, the colors in a red rose begin to emerge. As the light source increases, the color becomes brighter and more intense. The color of your car appears different on a dull and hazy day than on a bright and sunny day, and it looks different under some street lights than in sunlight. The brightness or dullness of a color partially depends on its light source.

You learned in the previous chapter that the lightness or darkness of colors or grays is called *value*. In a black-and-white photograph, it is easy to distinguish light gray and white areas (light values) from medium and dark-valued areas. White is the lightest value and black is the darkest value, with an unlimited number of values lying in between.

To emphasize the almost infinite number of values at our disposal, imagine placing one drop of ink into a ten-thousand-gallon tank of clear water. Stir well. With a small brush, make a swatch of this mixture on white paper. Now repeat: add one more drop of ink, stir, then place another swatch beside the first. Repeat over and over again. It might take years to finish, and the swatches might stretch from Florida to California. You would not be able to distinguish between the various values next to each other because their difference would be so slight.

It is easier to work with fewer values. Try using pencil, charcoal, or crayon to make a value chart that uses three values: light, medium, and dark. Then make a value chart that uses five values, and maybe one that uses ten values.

As you look at various black-and-white paintings and photographs in this book, notice the use of values. Notice how the artists make objects or people contrast with their surroundings by using contrasting values. Notice how moods can be established by using dark or light values. Notice that some paintings have very few value changes, while others make use of a wide range of values from brightest light to darkest black. The control of values is one of the most important aspects of an artist's craft.

Winslow Homer used a range of light values in most of his watercolor *Maine Cliffs* (1883). The distant dark water, trees, and birds become the accents in this high-keyed painting. Collection of the Brooklyn Museum, bequest of Sidney B. Curtis.

Medium and light values dominate *The Cliff at Morning, Ozarks* (1921) by Carl Rudolph Kraft. Notice the flat feeling achieved by using such similar values. A few darker values create contrast in the foreground. Collection of The Los Angeles County Museum of Art, Mr. and Mrs. William Preston Harrison Collection.

To make value changes in a color, you need to add white to make it lighter and black to make it darker. If you are using transparent watercolor, adding more water to the wash will thin it out, making the color lighter in value by letting the white paper show through the diluted color. You might want to make some value charts using color, mixing it with black and white paint for darker and lighter values.

Light Values

If an artist wishes to make a painting showing sunshine and warmth, what values do you think will be emphasized? The brighter the sunshine, the lighter the values will be. However, dark shadows will also be more defined. Think of the glare of bright sunshine at the beach or on white snow. The values are so light that we often put on sunglasses to darken them so that we can see more easily and clearly.

A painting with many light-valued colors is called a *high-keyed* painting, and the colors are often called *pastels.* They have white mixed with them, so they are lighter *tints* of the original color. Perhaps you can find photographs in magazines in which most of the colors are light in value.

There is a wide range of light-valued grays. When working with pencil, for example, it is necessary to distinguish between various gray values. Most of them have light values, because the darkest tone might be only a dark gray and not black. When shading with pencil, you are actually shading with values. Try making a pencil value chart that shows ten value changes, with the darkest value only a medium gray. Try drawing a single white object (pitcher, lamp, baseball, golf ball, statue) and shade it with pencil in many light-valued grays.

Cut one-inch-square swatches of light grays from magazines and arrange a chart showing value steps from white to medium gray. This will help you become aware of the wide variety of values available for artists to use.

Light-valued washes of oil paint were brushed onto a tagboard surface to create the delicate softness in this work. A few dark accents keep the surface from becoming too shallow. John Marshall High School, Los Angeles.

The paintings of Albert Pinkham Ryder usually are done with colors of very dark values. *The River* is no exception. The lighter-valued sky offers the only strong contrast. Collection of the Los Angeles County Museum of Art, Paul Rodman Mabury Collection.

The lightest value in Guy Wiggins' painting is a middle-valued gray, and the artist uses dark values all the way to black. Although *Spring Awakening* (1922) is done in full color, the black-and-white photograph illustrates the values that are present. Collection of the Los Angeles County Museum of Art, gift of Jo Ann and Julian Ganz, Jr.

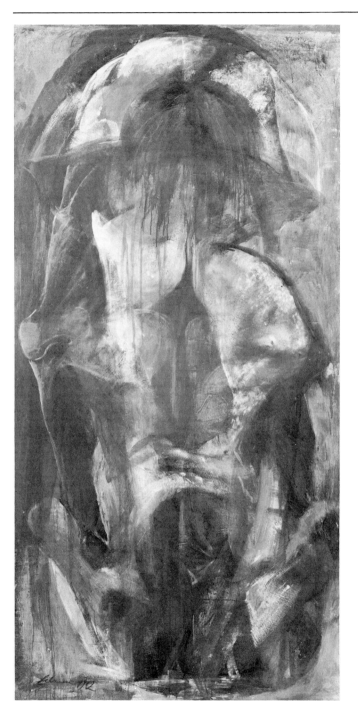

Dark Values

Dark and gloomy days, dusk, night, and dim light bring to mind certain types of paintings. These paintings often use dark values to set the mood. They might also use little contrast between values. As you know from Chapter 2, darker values of colors, or shades, have black added to them.

The value scale of grays can also range to darker values and eventually to black. Drawings and paintings that have primarily dark values are called *low-keyed*. If you draw and shade on a medium gray sheet of paper with black charcoal, the result will be low-keyed because all the values are dark, the lightest being the gray of the paper.

Find some black-and-white magazine pictures. Cut one-inch squares of dark gray values, from medium gray to black. Arrange them in an interesting way to show a value scale of dark-valued grays. Compare this scale with a similar light-valued scale to get an idea of the very wide range of gray values, extending from white to black.

The apparent lack of contrast between values, and an emphasis on darker values creates a somber, depressing mood in Rico Lebrun's casein painting, *Figure in the Flood* (1962). National Collection of Fine Arts, Smithsonian Institution, gift of S. C. Johnson and Son, Inc.

Strong value contrasts are evident when an inked wood block is printed on white paper. Lutheran High School, Los Angeles.

Value Contrast

While some photographs and paintings use all dark values or all light values, most artists like to work with a variety of values from all parts of the scale. You can make a very fine painting or drawing with only three, four, or five values, although some people might want to use many more. Many artists like to have their work show *value contrast*: light values are placed against medium or dark values and dark values against medium or light values. The contrast makes the parts easy to see and recognize. The greatest value contrast would be between black and white. If you have ever printed a linoleum cut or woodcut on white paper with black ink, you will recall that the contrast in such a print is very strong.

Not many painters work with such strong contrasts. Instead, many prefer to use the extremes (black and white) in small areas and use a range of values in most of the work. If you have difficulty seeing the values in a painting, squint your eyes to shut out tiny detail, and look at the larger shapes of similar value. When you do this, you are seeing the real composition of the painting, the large elements of dark and light that the artist used to construct the work.

Value contrast makes a work of art visually more exciting. Some artists reserve the most extreme contrast in their work for the center of interest, which is where the artist wants your eyes to land. Look at several paintings in this book and try to find the place where the lightest light and the darkest dark come together. Often (but not always) this area of greatest value contrasts will be the center of interest.

Paul Cézanne used middle values in most of this painting, but he sparked the surface with both dark and light accents. Notice how he used light against dark and dark against light in many places, to emphasize the forms. Cézanne was a master of visual design, and such a painting could appear in every chapter of this book to illustrate the various elements and principles of design. *Still Life* (26″ x 32⅜″). National Gallery of Art, Washington, D.C., The Chester Dale Collection.

Although the only color you see in this black and white reproduction of Vincent Van Gogh's pastel drawing is gray, the range of values helps you distinguish buildings, trees, fences, houses, sky and land. *View of an Industrial City* (15½″ x 21″). Stedelijk Museum, Amsterdam.

In a generally light-valued picture, a dark shape or line will be an accent or center of interest. In a generally dark-valued picture, a light shape will become most important. In a picture that uses four or five values, the area of greatest contrast will become visually most important.

It is interesting to work with *value relationships.* As with color value, a medium gray will appear lighter when placed in a dark area than it will in a lighter area. The effect of a gray value or color value changes with its surroundings. Cut out four one-inch-square swatches of medium gray, all the same value. Then cut out four larger swatches, each about three inches square, from white, black, and two different gray-valued papers, each different from the original gray swatches. As you place the small gray shapes on the four larger shapes, the value of the smaller shapes seems to change with each example, yet it actually is the same. This exercise should help you understand that the lightness and darkness of values really depend on their relationship to the values of things around them.

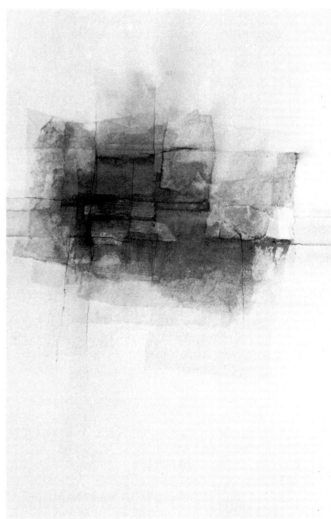

Barbara Weldon glued layer on layer of tissue paper in her untitled work. The more layers used, the darker the values become.

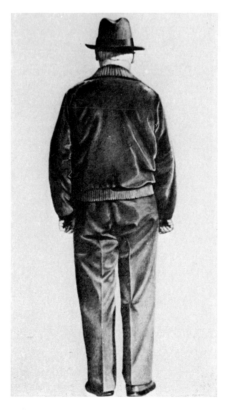

Man, a pencil drawing by Donald Hendricks, is 30 inches high. Notice how carefully the artist used a complete range of values, from very light gray to solid black. Such skillful shading requires a keen eye to notice subtle changes in value on the model.

The fluid watercolor technique of Robert E. Wood makes use of a complete range of values. Notice how the artist controlled his subject by placing light shapes against darker backgrounds and dark shapes against lighter areas. Can you find the center of interest by locating an area where lightest light and darkest dark are contrasting? *Cooks Bay, Moorea* (22" x 30").

Notice the value changes in Nick Follansbee's pencil drawing. The form of the model's face is described by the values of the pencil strokes. Can you determine the direction of the source of light?

Using Value to Show Depth

If you glance through the illustrations in Chapter 5, you will see how values can be used to describe three-dimensional space. Normally, objects in a landscape or cityscape painting get lighter in value as they recede in space. If an artist uses all light values or all dark values, the space may seem shallow. A complete range of values produces a feeling of more depth.

Drawing shadows creates values that show depth on a single object. Adding shading to an outlined circle, for example, can change it from a flat-looking shape to a rounded form. If the light is coming from a single source, the part of the object facing the light is lightest in value, and the part that receives the least light is darkest in value (see diagrams). If an object has sharp edges—like a box, book, or house—the change in value is sudden and sharp. If the object is round, the change in value is gradual.

Artists can use actual light sources when they draw or paint, or they can change the light and values to suit themselves. Light may come from left, right, above, behind, or ahead. Areas facing that light source will be shown as lightest in value; shadow areas will be darker. Sometimes an artist may wish to control the light and arrange lights and darks to emphasize certain aspects of the work. Such values would not be realistic, but would be used to strengthen the composition of the work.

The bold planes of dark, medium, and light values create a sense of space in this basically flat design. Roger Kuntz, *Freeway Series*, oil on canvas.

This photograph can be used to summarize the many aspects of value presented in this chapter. How many statements about value can you make, using this photograph as visual information?

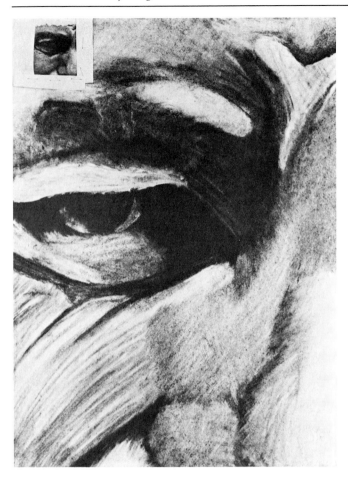

A student used part of a small black-and-white photograph (see upper left) as a source of information for this 24-inch x 18-inch charcoal drawing. A complete range of values is needed to show highlight and shadow. Even though the skin of the person is all one color, many values are needed to express depth, shadow, and light. Reseda High School, California.

Other Design Projects

Make a simple still life drawing on medium gray paper. The paper itself will provide the middle values. Add white chalk for the lighter values and black chalk or charcoal for the darker values.

Make a color value scale by starting with two puddles of a single color. Make swatches (or paint in ruled spaces) by adding a little more white in each case until the lightest value is reached. Start with the second puddle and add a little black each time until the darkest value is reached. Notice the changes that take place in the color from one end of the scale to the other.

Using a single color, plus black and white, make a monochromatic painting that incorporates at least seven different values. Do not have pure black or pure white in the painting, but use for the darkest and lightest values.

Explore the potential of creating different values with ground charcoal dust, using your thumbs and index fingers only. Overlapping areas will become darker in value.

Use three different values of colored paper cut from magazines. Glue them on a separate piece of paper, creating the illusion of space by location and overlapping.

Mix three ink washes of different value in three small containers, using varied amounts of water and ink. Try to paint a landscape, a still life, or a student model with these three values. Overlapping washes will create new and darker values. You might want to add an ink line for accent.

Use three ballpoint or marker pens of different colors—red, yellow, and blue—to suggest near, mid, and distant forms in a drawing. Use yellow for near forms and blue for distant forms.

Use only black and white tempera paint to make a painting that will use only value and no color. Try for a wide range of values. Reserve pure blacks and whites for the area of central interest.

Use a variety of media in black, gray, and white to create a mixed-media painting. Stress the variety of materials by emphasizing texture and value contrasts. Use media such as black ink, black and white crayons, black and white tempera or acrylics, black and white markers, pencils, black and white paper.

Explore moods or meanings that may be expressed with values, attempting to illustrate one-word themes such as hunger, tragedy, loss, peace, happiness, jazz, carnival.

Cut out a photograph of an active sports figure. Trace the *outline* of the figure on one side of a sheet of paper. Draw lines around the figure that make spaces get wider as they go toward the edges (see the example of the runner on this page). Constrict the shapes in some places to add interest and variety. Paint the spaces with progressive value changes, starting with a light value and working toward black. A sensation of vibration should develop.

Three values of ink washes (light, medium, and dark) plus black ink for the line are used in this student wash drawing. Overlapping washes in many places darken values and help create the illusion of form. Lutheran High School, Los Angeles.

A single running figure seems to vibrate with energy as value changes darken as they radiate toward the outer edges of the paper.

Another of the visual elements is *shape*. Shapes are enclosed areas, solid matter that tells us that something is an apple, or a cloud, or a person. We readily identify objects by the shapes they present.

Many people use the term *shape* to describe three-dimensional form, but *form* is a more accurate description. Whereas shape is only two-dimensional, form is three-dimensional: it has length, width, and depth. Forms imply weight and solidity; shapes suggest a single surface.

Shape and form are used in most art expression. Artists, architects, sculptors, and designers all use shapes and forms to create their visual ideas: perhaps two-dimensional paintings and advertising designs (shapes) or three-dimensional pieces of sculpture or buildings (forms). In this chapter we will emphasize the important visual qualities of shapes and forms that will help sharpen your perceptions and give you a keener eye and new insights on how shapes and forms affect us.

Shape and Form

Categories of Shapes

In the following discussion we refer specifically to shapes. However, in most cases, the same information may also be applied to forms.

A starting point is to become aware of the types of shapes we encounter. Shapes fit easily into two basic categories: *geometric* and *organic*. Certain geometric shapes are easy to recognize, such as the circle, the square, or the triangle. You may even be familiar with more complex geometric shapes, like pentagons or hexagons.

The geometric shape is precise and sharply defined. Most manufactured and person-made products are based on geometric shapes. We see such shapes in architecture and product design. Nature also shows us many geometric shapes and forms. A tree trunk can be seen as a cylinder and an orange as a sphere. Try making a few simplified drawings or diagrams of your surroundings using geometric shapes to interpret complex subject matter.

Although we often recognize geometric shapes in nature, most natural objects are organic shapes. Organic shapes reflect the free-flowing aspects of growth and are produced in a wide variety of precise and irregular shapes. You might try making a line

Painting involves judgments about the placement of shapes
to create appealing space division, as well as using shapes
to describe subject matter. Pablo Picasso, *Courtesan with
Jewelled Collar,* oil on canvas (21" x 25"). Los Angeles
County Museum of Art, Mr. and Mrs. George Gard de Sylva
Collection.

This skyscraper in San Francisco is based on geometric forms. Rectangular windows fit into triangular sides, which combine to produce a tall pyramid.

Organic forms have a moving quality, and this section of rocky landscape captures the moving rhythms of irregular forms.

Solid massive forms provide a feeling of strength and power, as in this cast bronze sculpture of a horse by Marino Marini.

drawing of an organic design that reflects the qualities of growth we see in nature. Your lines should flow and express the movement of a shape.

By analyzing geometric and organic shapes, you should see the obvious differences and similarities. Some shapes are curved or round, others straight or angular. Some are solid, some are open. There are even shapes between shapes.

Curved and Angular Shapes

Many shapes can be simply described as curved or curvilinear (thin curved outlines of shapes), or angular. Curved shapes are graceful; angular shapes suggest strength. We tend to see curves rapidly as the eye sweeps along a form uninterruptedly. A series of repeated curves sets up a rhythmical pattern. On the other hand, angular shapes are straight-edged and lean away from a vertical position. This leaning position suggests movement and increases the shape's

power. Looking at angular shapes, the eye moves along the shape and stops momentarily where one shape connects with another. Patterns of angular shapes create a structural quality; opposing shapes produce visual tension.

To capture the feeling of these contrasting shapes, use drawing media to explore several designs that are constructed with either curved or angular shapes. Using mechanical devices such as rulers, compasses, french curves, and triangles, build linear designs that are totally curved or totally angular.

Three-dimensional angular structures are expressive ways to capture the power of angular forms. Try using wooden sticks, cardboard strips, or folded paper strips adhered with white glue. Study the work of artists such as Lyonel Feininger, Franz Kline, and Wassily Kandinsky to see the use of curved and angular shapes to express visual qualities in paint.

Curved forms provide a feeling of gracefulness, and these two handsomely designed bookends by Al Ching take the curved forms of a rainbow and clouds and transform them into a utilitarian purpose.

Positive and Negative Shapes

Just as the positive and negative parts of a battery work together to produce electrical current, so do positive and negative shapes function as a visual unit. Positive shapes are the solid, tangible aspects of a composition. Negative shapes are the areas that either surround the shape or exist between shapes. All seeing, therefore, entails viewing both these elements—positive shape always has a negative counterpart. If you spread the fingers of your hand, the positive shapes would be your fingers and thumb, and the negative shapes or spaces would be between your fingers.

For the artist, negative shapes are as important as positive shape in a composition. In placing shapes within a composition or format (the total shape used for arranging), you should carefully consider the effective amounts of positive versus negative shapes. You should view each negative shape as a unique part of the composition, not as an incidental part of a background. Often a painter or designer will start by working the negative shapes first. Painting the shapes around and between subject matter produces the areas of positive shapes more thoughtfully.

The silhouetted shape (shape without detail or modeling) presents a strong statement of positive and negative shapes. Try squinting at shapes to lose the distracting details and to see the shapes, positive and negative, more effectively as areas of a composition. Then you can see the importance of positive and negative working together as interlocking parts. After trying this exercise, explore the idea with art media. Start by composing with positive and negative shapes cut from black paper. These cut pieces can depict subject matter such as still life forms, or they can be abstract areas. Move the positive black shapes into a variety of positions, looking at the interesting kinds of negative shapes you can produce.

Try drawing a still life by first putting in all the negative shapes. Use a cut-out viewfinder (a small cardboard frame) to search for effective positive and negative shape arrangements. Once you have found a pleasing composition of shapes, you can sketch the basic shapes. These sketches can be useful for future drawings, paintings, or designs.

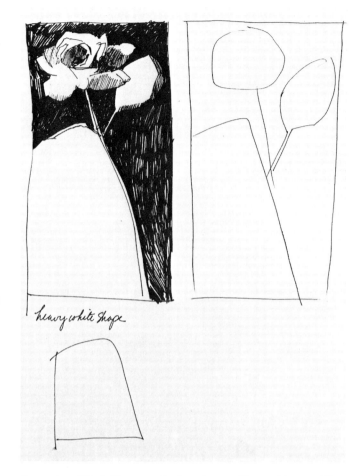

heavy white shape

Even simplified diagramatic drawings will consider positive and negative shape relationships. Kim Williams' sketch analyzes the interaction between positive and negative shapes.

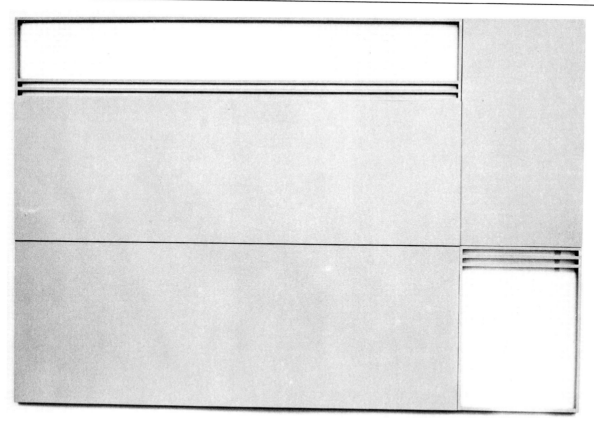

Artist Claude Kent used wood, glass, and enamel to produce this art piece. Careful consideration was given to the most effective amounts of positive shapes (gray shapes) and negative shapes (white areas).

Angular forms are often used when forceful designs are desired. This welded sculpture opposes one form against the next to create a sense of energy and strength.

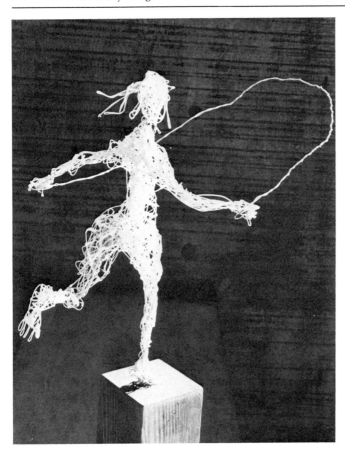

Wire is an ideal medium to capture the feeling of movement and both lightness and heaviness. The massing of wire produces solidity and weight.

Open sculpture is an ideal example of positive and negative forms functioning together. Assembling a sculpture from cut or fabricated pieces will increase your awareness of how carefully positioned forms can make positive and negative forms work effectively.

Qualities of Shapes

Light and Heavy Shapes

Understanding the important qualities of shapes means making effective sensory assessments. These judgments cover a wide range of human responses. Our five senses—sight, hearing, taste, touch, and smell—provide the significant data. We know an apple is hard and crisp by touching it, tasting it, and even just by looking at it.

Looking at shapes and forms can provide innumerable clues about the nature of an object, how it functions, how its surface would feel, what it would taste like if edible, and how pleasing it is to view. Investigations add to our experiences and heighten our visual pleasure. Some characteristics that help us to identify the shapes and forms are surface, weight and mass, material composition, and position in space.

When we draw or construct shapes, we need to understand how to interpret qualities such as lightness or heaviness. There should be a striking difference in the line quality or value contrasts between rendering a cloud and rendering a rock or a mountain form. Soft, floating clouds would require a lighter touch, a subtle blending of values and diffused edges. On the other hand, rocks and mountains demand a strong, hard surface quality. This type of description would need strong value contrasts and more powerful line. Try drawing two objects of approximately the same size, one light and soft, the other heavy and solid. By using descriptive values and line contrasts, see if you can capture the object's quality. Also try exploring three-dimensional forms with qualitative differences. Wire or string can suggest airiness and delicacy; plaster, clay, or wood can convey feelings of solidity and weight.

You will see that interpreting the qualities of shapes with art media helps affirm your visual experiences. It also makes you able to portray convincingly all kinds of forms where weight description is an important consideration.

Alberto Giacometti's elongated thin sculpture *Tall Figure, 1* (Norton Simon Pasadena Museum of Art) contrasts with Gaston Lachaise's solid, heavy forms used to depict human structure (U.C.L.A.'s Franklin Murphy sculpture garden).

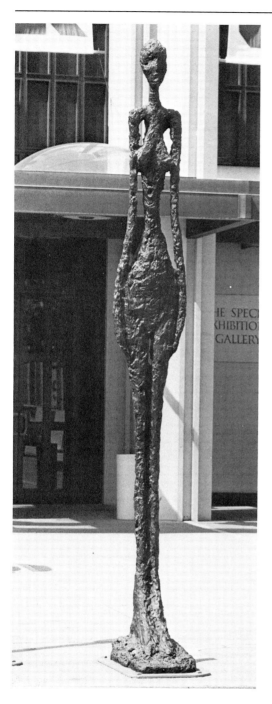

Smooth and Textured Shapes

The surface of a shape is one quality that not only informs but also delights the eye. Visually experiencing smooth, textured surfaces is often linked with past tactile encounters with forms. For the sightless, this tactile experience translates important impressions from fingers to brain.

Smooth surfaces readily identify with certain objects. Both eyes and fingers can move easily across glass, finished wood, polished metal, and plastic surfaces. Textured surfaces, particularly those with high relief (extensions of shapes above the surface level) slow down the visual-tactile experience. Thus when we look at objects, smooth surfaces allow for quick scanning; textured surfaces impede the eye speed and slow down our observation.

Light strongly affects the surface qualities of shapes. A smooth, light-valued surface will reflect light easily. A similar light-valued surface that is textured will absorb light and reflect far less. Shiny, smooth surfaces are highly reflective; textured surfaces are duller.

Rubbings, made with pencil or crayon, over a variety of surfaces can describe surfaces. From these experiments you can create collages, using both found and simulated surfaces. One can then explore the effects of closely positioned smooth and textured surfaces. Certain objects can be transformed into eerie or surrealistic forms by changing textural surfaces. The Dadaists employed this when they made objects like fur-lined teacups. Our psychological responses are heightened by seeing such unusual effects.

Shapes can be made appealing by emphasis on their surface qualities. Artists and craftspeople are very conscious of the visual appeal created by careful attention to surface qualities. As viewers, we can appreciate their efforts. We also can extend our own sensitivities to the wide range of natural and human objects that have unique surfaces.

Gather a number of intriguing textural surfaces, such as tree bark, crushed paper, or various seeds, and make a texture board by gluing areas of textured shapes to a board. These can be placed into geometric or free-flowing designs to provide an organized format.

A number of drawings can be made to closely simulate both smooth and textured surfaces. Other simulated textures might use more involved media, such as watercolor, tempera, and mixed media.

Static and Dynamic Shapes

How a shape or form is positioned in space can generate a force or create a feeling of repose and stability. A leaning shape can give an impression of visual strength and the feel of action. Both vertical and horizontal positions stabilize the visual qualities of forms. We associate the leaning shape with movement, as in running and climbing, and the lack of action with standing still or resting.

Static shapes will produce a peaceful landscape composition. Horizontal and vertical shapes, such as trees and landforms, can imply stability. When a more active or dynamic scene is desired, then leaning shapes and swirling clouds will produce a moving quality and dynamic activity. Vincent Van Gogh's paintings are primarily dynamic because he positioned shapes to create this sense of movement.

Most building shapes are static, for they are generally vertical and horizontal in position. The forces of nature produce dynamic shapes, such as seen in wind-blown clouds, eroded mountains, trees bent over by a strong gale, or the action of humans and animals.

Artists imply action by shifting shapes into diagonal or off-center positions. Whether they use flat shapes or three-dimensional forms (as in sculpture), the effect is the same.

Try putting together two small paper sculptures, one in a static position and the other in a dynamic arrangement.

Make a static cityscape from cut paper that is totally composed of vertical and horizontal shapes. Contrast this compositional feeling with a dynamic composition of angled shapes.

When a form leans away from the vertical static position, a sense of movement is created. This tree form is further activated by swirling grain patterns.

Metal sculpture is often formed and finished to emphasize a smooth, shiny surface, which is pleasing to both the eye and the hand.

Form and Light

All seeing depends on light, either artificial light or natural light. Light's impact on shapes and form is phenomenal. We all have witnessed how crisp, well-defined landforms change to dark, flat silhouetted shapes as the sun sets. There is a sharp difference between the light at sunrise and sunset and the light that dazzles us at noon.

The power and angle of the light are what define the forms we see. The French Impressionist painter Claude Monet devoted countless hours to outdoor painting at specific periods of the day. He would study and paint the same haystack or cathedral only when the light was defining forms in the precise way it was on his previous painting trips. He wanted a particular *impression* of form, imposed by a consistent quality of light. Artists today are just as enamored by light and its effects. In fact, light itself can be the media. It creates shapes and forms by bouncing on certain surfaces.

Different surfaces reflect light differently. A light, polished surface will reflect most of the light it receives. A dark, dull, textured surface will absorb the major portion of light and give minimal reflective power. Artists and craftspeople choose surface qualities that match the expression they want to make. One sculptor may want a sleek, polished form that casts light in many directions; another may want a rough, cut form that modulates light in a suppressed way. Dark black shapes in a painting sharply contrast lighter shapes. The darks in paintings showing objects close up tend to recede, the lights to jump forward. In distant landscape paintings, the opposite is often true. Rembrandt's paintings are excellent examples of the use of controlled light to increase the power of painted forms. Light conditions all the forms we see around us and to a degree, the forms condition the effects of light. Light changes gradually on round or curved forms but suddenly on angular and sharp-edged forms.

The use of illuminated light shapes and mirrored surfaces in a department store produces a highly active design. This is one approach in using light to produce a unique wall and ceiling pattern.

It is intriguing to produce art objects with varying surfaces and angles, and then cast lights on them to dramatize their forms. You can try this with simple sculptural forms, or even with folded or pleated paper.

Shadow shapes carry a type of dark and light message. A shadow can mirror the form it is created from, or be distorted into more intriguing shapes. Complex shadow patterns, such as we might get from a rack of bicycles, are challenging drawing or painting subjects. Try experimenting with just black and white compositions that reflect viewed shadow shapes in your home or neighborhood.

Light is a powerful design agent that has a strong impact on the shapes and forms we see, as well as those we work with artistically. Because the mastery of light is critical to the mastery of form, you should make every effort to understand and duplicate its qualities.

Rembrandt was a master of dark and light. This etching explores form by overlaying lines to create value changes. *Christ Preaching*, 1652. National Gallery of Art, Washington, D.C., Gift of W.G. Russell Allen.

Seeing Shapes as Design

Knowing the elements and principles of design can drastically change the way you look at your visual world. Instead of merely using your sight for identifying things or for making functional decisions, you can discover a constantly fascinating environment of design. Instead of viewing buildings as stores, factories, or homes, look instead at the design of their forms, their rhythmical patterns, and their extensions into space. Then you will start to observe as if you are thinking in terms of a painting, a collage, or a three-dimensional design. A stack of dishes becomes a repeated pattern of shapes; a line of telephone poles, a design of interacting positive and negative shapes; and a trip to the supermarket, a panorama of designed arrangements.

This newer seeing experience will be reinforced by, and will in turn reinforce, the art you produce. The more you can see as artists, the easier it is to use your remembered vision when you draw, paint, or construct forms. All great painters are careful observers. They reflect their environments as well as their feelings. They use their sight to pick out all the significant design or compositional material they can find.

The process of discovery can start close at hand or cover a wide territory. You might start by surveying things around the house—kitchen utensils, the telephone, a bookcase, furniture shapes and room arrangements, chests of drawers, or lighting fixtures. By looking at objects from several perspectives, you will see different shapes. Try looking straight down on an object, or below it, or at an unusual angle. Visually frame each viewing to make a small composition. Make small, quick sketches of the most impressive views to help increase your design awareness.

Design possibilities are endless outdoors. It is easy to be overpowered by too much visual material, so good technique is to focus on sections of the visual field. This process is similar to the procedure of skilled photographers who select subject matter and try different viewpoints. Once they see the most appealing composition, they snap the picture.

Try taking part of a landscape—your backyard, a group of store fronts, or a gas station. Walk around the area to pinpoint sections that produce strong design qualities. What are the ingredients that make this

Looking at sections of familiar forms reveals new design properties. The telephone receiver, cord, and shadows all contribute to an effective visual composition.

particular section intriguing? Is it the variety of shapes, the grouping of shapes, or the contrast and interaction of shapes?

Undoubtedly, the close-up view provides some of the most unique design experiences: plants, flowers, weeds, trees, leaves, insects, wall surfaces, fences, doors, sections of fruit and vegetables, sea shells, and rocks. A general view passes over most of these. Concentrate on just part of an object and look for the minute shapes—the veins of leaves, the bark of the tree, or the grain of a piece of wood. Use magnifying glass to zero in on the tiniest detail. Try drawing these close-up views. It will give you a good start on building a reference file for future designs.

The enjoyment of seeing in the fullest sense reflects our understanding of visual elements and principles. As we grasp the significance of shape and form, we can apply that knowledge to a more invigorating visual world.

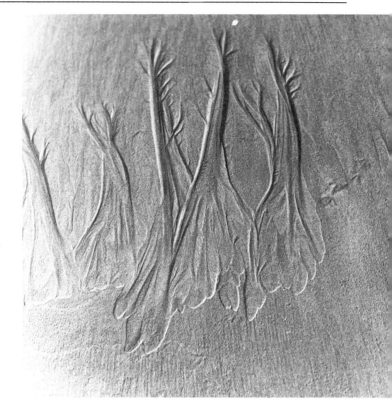

Close-up views, such as these sand patterns at the beach, offer fresh ideas for designs.

Explore the design possibilities of ordinary objects by selective seeing, photographing, or drawing. Villa Park High School, California.

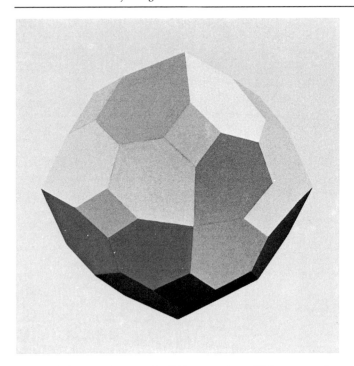

Try modeling a shape with different values. This geometric shape was treated with seven distinct values to produce a solid angular form.

Other Design Projects

Since shape and form are basic to each area of art, you can select from a wide range of activities to experience these art elements. Shape problems will involve two dimensions. Therefore, they are ideal for drawing, painting, printmaking, and design. Form naturally lends itself to three-dimensional media, such as clay, wood, formed paper, papier-mâché, plaster, wire, and metal. Each activity may suggest other avenues of expressing the same idea, which you should explore if they seem promising.

Find objects that approximate any geometric form (such as oranges for spheres or cans for cylinders). Draw these objects using only geometric shapes.

Try to draw an organic irregular shape by using just geometric shapes to interpret the form.

Construct several geometric forms out of paper. Arrange them in a still life. Put a strong single light source on the forms, then make a drawing in soft lead or charcoal that shows both shape and rendered form. including cast shadow.

Draw a group of figures or objects, linking all shapes so that the total unit becomes one major shape.

Take a single letter shape and reproduce it five to eight times in several variations. Some sections of the design (drawn, painted, or cut out), can be partial details of the letter. Let some parts overlap to form new shapes.

Make the shape of a word express its meaning by exaggeration (stretching and compressing the shape), by using an angled position, or with rhythmical movement.

Produce a landscape painting using only silhouetted shapes. Vary the values to separate foreground, middle-distance, and background areas. Black, gray, and white paper can be substituted for paint.

Build a tower or building using applicator sticks, balsa wood, or folded paper strips. Start with a designed module form (a particular geometric form) and repeat this form in a variety of sizes and placements. Several solid panels can be adhered to selected parts to contrast open and closed forms.

Using softened wire (annealed, galvanized, or copper), create a solid-looking mass that captures the action of an animal or human. You can use several thicknesses of wire to suggest the different weights of the body and limbs.

Roll out a number of clay slabs. Cut them into a series of shapes that relate to each other (all curved, all straight, all angled). After the pieces dry firmly, build a sculptural piece that uses space as an important design element. Extend some pieces away from a central core and balance with opposing shapes. Adhere pieces by scoring edges and using clay slip as a binder. After the piece is thoroughly dried, fire it in a kiln.

Start a scrapbook of selected photos or clippings. This can be a starting point in discovering many of the design aspects of both static and dynamic shapes and forms.

The sense of space is accomplished in a number of ways in this painting by Gabe Kreiswirth. The bright red chair contrasts with the soft, diffused handling of the wall and floor, the clothing on the figure contrasts with the chair, and the arms of the figure and the shape of the chair present a strong, centrally located circular form that almost seems to move. Courtesy of Orlando Gallery, Encino, California.

The artist used broad brushstrokes and areas of color to preserve the flatness of the picture plane. A sense of space is accomplished through lines and shapes running from the foreground toward the high horizon line. Richard Diebenkorn, *Cityscape*, 1963, oil on canvas (60½" x 52½"). Courtesy of San Francisco Museum of Modern Art. Purchased with contributions of Trustees and Friends in memory of Hector Escobosa, Brayton Wilbur and J.D. Zellerbach.

Space

Space, sometimes crowded, sometimes open, is all around you. It may be full of trees or buildings, clouds, or clear air. It can be contained by walls or open to the horizons. We run, walk, and drive in space. When you walked to the shelf to pick up this book, you were walking in space. The words *forward, back, around, under, behind, over, into,* and *out from* all indicate action taken in space.

Two-Dimensional Space

Flat items—the floor, a table top, a sheet of cardboard—can be described in terms of two dimensions, height and width. They have no depth. A 12-inch x 18-inch flat sheet of paper has no depth, so it is two-dimensional. We could fold the paper to make it three-dimensional, or we might draw on it to produce an illusion of some three-dimensional form. But the *flat* sheet of paper is simply a two-dimensional surface.

Positive and Negative Space

We can extend our earlier discussion of positive and negative shapes to apply to space. If you put a black square on the flat white paper, you get a new feeling. The surface is still two-dimensional, but it is now divided into black and white spaces. The black square is a positive shape and the white background area around it is a negative space. If you add a few more black shapes, the feeling will change. You will see several black positive spaces and an encompassing white negative space.

Generally, bolder color spaces will appear positive against a more neutral background. At times it is difficult to tell which space is positive and which is negative. In fact, some artists (such as Escher) take pleasure in deceiving the eye by creating optical illusions with positive and negative space.

The Picture Plane

The surface on which an artist works—whether it be paper, board, canvas, or fiberboard—is called the *picture plane*. Since *plane* means flat, it is two-dimensional. It is difficult to create much actual depth on a canvas. Van Gogh managed to create depth with thick applications of paint (impasto). A collage artist might build up a surface with paper, fabric, or cardboard.

In this lettering design, depth is achieved in a number of ways. Some letters and words are smaller than others, thereby seeming farther away; some overlap others that also create a sense of depth; the darker letters advance visually, while the lighter letters seem to recede.

Artists sometimes cut or tear the canvas as part of their working method, but most drawings and paintings are flat.

When painters want their work to have a three-dimensional effect they manipulate the media and the elements of art to produce a sense of depth. Even so, the picture plane remains flat.

When flat shapes just touch each other on the picture plane, the space seems compressed and a flatness is felt, because no depth is experienced. Overlapping the shapes produces a feeling of depth because it appears as if one shape is in front of the other. Outlined shapes tend to appear flat when there are no shadows or when no shading appears on the shapes. Calligraphy and lettering also seem to produce a two-dimensional feeling.

Try these ideas yourself. Use the *same* objects in each picture—perhaps fruit or leaves or bottles. Cut the shapes from paper and place them on a contrasting sheet of paper. Don't let the pieces touch each other. Then arrange them so they just barely touch at their edges. Try overlapping some of the pieces. Notice the sense of flatness or three-dimensional effects that occur in each arrangement.

Flatness Produced by Closely Related Values, Colors, and Patterns

When values (darks and lights) are closely related, space appears to be flattened. None of the shapes seems to exert itself, to move forward or backward, and the design remains two-dimensional.

Closely related colors (all containing one common color) will do the same thing. Orange, yellow-orange, and red-orange shapes, if they are nearly the same in value, will tend to lie flat on the picture plane. Contrasting colors will show depth because the warmer and brighter colors will seem to come forward.

A picture plane covered with pattern eliminates a feeling of depth. Repeating shapes, lines, or colors in a regular system develops a strong two-dimensional feeling. If designers want to emphasize flatness, they can use both close-valued patterns and related colors.

You might want to try this as a class experiment or extra project. Choose three closely related colors of paper. Cut out similar shapes, perhaps squares or rectangles, from each of the colors. Paste them on another surface, completely covering it. Notice that the related colors make the picture seem relatively flat. Now choose a contrasting color, cut a few similar shapes, and put them over some of the shapes in your design. Observe what happens to the visual sense of space or dimension.

The Illusion of Depth in Art

By using many of the techniques described in the following pages, you can create a sense of three dimensions on a flat picture plane. Artists have been using startlingly similar methods of creating such depth for many centuries.

You have seen that overlapping flat shapes suggest a third dimension, depth. For example, look at the city scene on this page. As you look down the street, curb, sidewalk, and street lines converge in the distance. Size variation also shows depth: objects of similar size appear smaller when they are farther away, and objects such as lamp posts *seem* to get smaller and closer together. Objects closer to us overlap some that are farther away, and closer objects and surfaces are more detailed and defined than those far away. Finally, objects and shapes placed *higher* on the page seem farther away.

If a painting or drawing were done from this scene, the feeling of depth could be suggested through knowledge of the concepts discussed in this section.

Three-Dimensional Space

When we use words like *into, over, under, around, behind,* or *surrounding,* we are speaking of three-dimensional space. Another dimension, depth, has literally been added to the two-dimensional plane. This three-dimensional realm includes solidity, volume, and mass. We can physically walk *around* a three-dimensional sculpture or building.

Yet we should not be concerned *only* with the object we create or view. We should also notice its surrounding, or negative, space. When we walk around a three-dimensional sculpture, we are walking in the space that surrounds it. That space is a vital part of the object itself.

Space Around Things

Solid forms such as buildings, flagpoles, or monolithic mountains are three-dimensional and occupy *space.* We can move around them. We are not often conscious of the space surrounding such solid objects, especially if that space seems unlimited. When it is contained, as in a stadium or skyscraper-lined street, we become more aware of it. We become acutely aware of it when it is filled with smog, dust, or fog, all of which create an effect of solid space.

Space Flowing Through Things

Three-dimensional forms that are constructed with wire or pierced with holes will be penetrated by space. Air actually becomes an integral part of the structures or forms by occupying their interior spaces. Holes connect one side of the form with the other side. Our eyes move into, around, and out of the open spaces so that the shapes of these spaces become important to the form itself. A balanced relationship develops: space invades the form and the form occupies its surrounding space.

Irregular organic spaces occupy the areas between the branches of this tree. Air flows through and around the form and seems not to be contained by it because of the protrusions the tree makes in its surrounding space.

Solid sculptures of varied size or material exist in space. Space surrounds them, sometimes not quite penetrating their mass. Consider this negative space as an important part of sculpture. Try thinking of the shape of the space as much as the form of the sculpture or building. Sculpture by Henry Moore.

Space flows through and around the form of the trombone but cannot penetrate the human form itself. The positioning of the fingers can produce forms that can be punctured by space.

The bold, geometric shapes, by contrasting in dark and light, and overlapping each other, create a sense of space. The freer, fuzzier forms seem farther away, and the neutral background seems still farther. The artist, Stephen Seemayer, used an interesting technique of fire carbon drawing. Courtesy of Orlando Gallery, Encino, California.

Woven baskets have a textured surface, indicating shallow space.

Shadows indicate the depth of the space on the cast surface of this building. Though the design is abstract, the artist had the same concern with shallow space (low relief) as the sculptors who worked on the Parthenon in Athens.

Deep Space

The depth or shallowness of space is relative. A foot is deeper than an inch, but a mile is deeper than a foot. You can see depth when objects of a known size, such as mountains, skyscrapers, or people, seem tiny in the distance. We *know* they are far away, so the smaller they appear, the deeper the space. Pictures of the earth taken from outer space make the earth look like a Ping-Pong ball. We know that the depth of space is tremendous because we know that the actual size of the earth is huge.

Often objects of a known size seen in the foreground help to create the illusion of deep space because they give a sense of scale to the total scene. The great contrast in size between objects closer and farther away creates a strong feeling of depth because we *know* that space is between us and the more distant objects.

A small shape placed on a blank background may suggest great space, such as would occur in a photo of the earth taken from outer space. A similar effect may be achieved by placing a shape of bold color on a large, empty, and delicately colored background. The bolder shape will seem to advance away from the background, thereby emphasizing the sense of vast space.

Shallow Space

Ancient Greek artists who sculpted frieze figures used shallow space to great advantage. So do contemporary sculptors who work in *low relief*. Like deep space, shallow space is relative. It can vary from the crack in a brick to a window in a wall to a theater stage. You can easily contrast the shallow space of a bookshelf with the much deeper space of a city block.

We can often identify shallow spaces because of the shadows that are cast in them. When the light changes, the sense of space might disappear and then the surface would tend to become flat.

Protrusions above any surface into the surrounding shallow space produce a roughness, or texture, that can be felt. Depressions into any surface allow space to enter the surface; they also produce texture.

Congested Space

In the modern world, we are probably more aware of space that is filled with something than of space that seems empty. City spaces are crowded with buildings and people. Roadways and other driving spaces are choked with automobiles. Our living spaces are filled with furniture and our wall spaces are decorated with posters and memorabilia. The space under the hood of a car contains a variety of things to make the car run.

When you walk into a forest, you are not really conscious of the space the whole forest occupies, but only of the space *between* the trees or shrubs. Walking into an elevator with other people makes you aware of the lack of openness—the fullness of the enclosed area. It is congested, or filled, space.

Getting very close to some things might give you the feeling of congestion because you can see the many parts that they are constructed of. Yet a tree or tractor in a large open space can almost appear lonely. Artists may capture the sense of congestion by actually showing congested situations or by using colors, shapes, and lines in abstract or even non-objective ways to suggest congestion.

Looking into Spaces

Space is not only *around* things, it is also *inside* things. Often, when we look into some form or object, we cannot see inner details because the space inside looks dark or even black. That is because the light source has not reached this interior space and it appears dark by contrast with the outside of the form.

Shadows can also help define the shape of inside space. Curved shadows indicate a round form, while window and door frames cast straight-edged shadows. When light is not directly from the sun or other single strong light source, the edge of the shadows might seem soft, with a gradual change from light to dark.

At night, the inside space of a house appears much lighter than the dark spaces outside because it is illuminated artificially. If you become aware of the changes in value, you will find it easier to paint or draw the interior space.

Here is a fine example of interior light with dark surroundings. You may want to try the same thing, using subject
matter familiar to you. Lawrence Burchard, *Two Houses*,
1977, watercolor (28″ x 31″).

Looking down into a circular stairwell (there is a fountain
at the bottom), you see the values getting darker the deeper
you look.

Romare Bearden, one of America's finest collagists, shows a
crowded street scene. By not using realistic size relations
among objects and people, the congested, active look is exaggerated. *On Such a Night as This*, 1975. Collection of Cor-
bier-Ekstrom Gallery, New York.

This museum corridor is a fine example of one-point perspective. Imagine a white dot as the vanishing point in the black square at the end of the walk-way.

Rectangular boxcars are standing at an angle to the direction of the camera, so two vanishing points are evident. Since the eye level is above the top edge of the photo, you see the tops of the cars.

Although this high school student's watercolor does not use exact perspective (which could have lessened the liveliness of the scene), two-point perspective does exist. Can you find where?

Perspective

Linear Perspective: One-Point

Showing three-dimensional space on a two-dimensional surface (such as a painting or drawing) is *perspective.* Using lines to show depth produces *linear perspective.*

During the Renaissance, Italian artists discovered that when parallel straight lines move away from the observer, they seem to converge at a point in the distance. We call this point the *vanishing point* because it is where the objects seem to disappear. As mentioned earlier, these converging lines suggest depth.

Close one eye and you can see just like the camera lens. Observe the converging lines all around you as you look along a wall of lockers, up the side of a building, or along the street on the way home.

Linear perspective is a much used art technique, but it is still one of the best ways to show depth in drawing and painting.

Linear Perspective: Two-Point

While one-point perspective uses lines that lead to a single point and shows objects that are square with your line of sight, two-point perspective can deal with objects sitting at odd angles with your eye. The receding parallel lines seem to converge at two points set far apart.

Books, boxes, benches, or buildings that are at an angle with your line of sight can be shown in this way. When objects are drawn in correct perspective, you can feel the sense of space and depth. The eye level, or *horizontal line* (an imaginary line that represents your eye level when you look straight ahead) is shown by drawing a line parallel to the top edge of your paper. The vanishing points are located on the horizon line.

Systems for correctly depicting such spatial concepts can become quite complicated. If you look carefully at the way edges and lines slope and slant, you are well on your way to observing the cues that create perspective—the feeling of three-dimensional space.

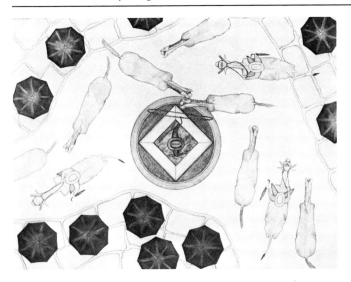

In this colored pencil drawing, the horses, figures, and umbrellas are shown from a direct overhead view—a difficult and fascinating job for the artist. Michael Ansell, *Park Series #3*, 1976. Courtesy of Orlando Gallery, Encino, California.

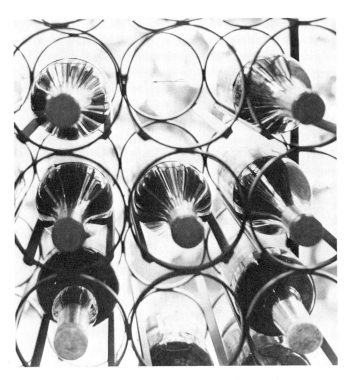

Both the bottles and the wine rack provide excellent examples of cylinders viewed from different angles. The top bottles are *at* eye level, while the bottom row is *below* eye level.

A Point of View: Looking At, Up at, or Down on Things

A building appears different from the street than from the roof next door because the angle or point of view determines how it will appear in space. Your car looks different when it is on the grease rack because you are not used to looking up at it. A baseball field looks different when you are standing on the pitcher's mound than when you are looking down on it from the stands. A mountain looks huge when you are at its base, but the valley looks smaller when you are on top of the mountain.

Look around carefully and try to see what happens to objects or people when you change your point of view. When you look down from a high window, for example, people walking on the street look quite different than they would if you were on the street, too. When you look straight down on a round plate, it is circular. But when you look at the same plate obliquely or from an angular point of view, it no longer seems perfectly round, but rather a flattened oval. How flat it appears depends on your eye level; the closer it is to your eye level, the flatter the oval looks.

Conventional spatial relationships change as your angle or point of view changes. Artists or photographers can take advantage of this to produce dramatic or provocative spatial concepts. Baroque artists, such as Correggio, Tiepolo and Rubens, and the Mannerist painters, such as Parmigianino, Tintoretto and El Greco, delighted in depicting things from peculiar points of view.

The Effect of Light on Space

Light is necessary for three-dimensional space to be seen correctly. As with color, if light is not present or is diffused or filtered, depth may seem flattened or nonexistent.

You can see three-dimensional space most accurately when the light source (the sun or a light bulb) is above or to the side of an object. You can also sense quite correctly when the light source is behind you. In all these cases, the objects will throw shadows that will help your eyes read the depth and space.

When the source of light is behind the object being viewed and is shining *at* you, it is called *back lighting*. Back lighting tends to flatten space. When you look *at* a sunset (the source of light), objects between you and the sun become flattened silhouettes.

The less light, the flatter the objects and space become. Even diffused light through fog or thick clouds creates a flatter look than full sunlight would produce. Dusk or dawn are difficult times to drive your car because accurate depth perception is hindered by the lack of light.

This fine painting emphasizes the flattening effect of space in rain and fog. Winn Jones, *Rain Images,* watercolor. Collection of Ms. Diane Skamfer.

Shadows and Space

Insufficient light tends to flatten space and an abundance of light emphasizes space. Because bright light causes objects in its path to cast shadows, our eyes read the results as space between object and shadow.

Shadows make a ball look *round* to us (so it occupies space). Sunlight and shadow give *form* to a tree, giving it volume. We can sense texture and shallow relief because of surface shadows.

An airplane flying overhead on a sunny day casts a shadow on the ground. A moth makes a darting shadow on the wall. Your body creates a recognizable shadow on the sidewalk. Generally, the closer the object is to the wall or ground, the sharper the shadow. The flying airplane casts a fuzzy shadow, while your own shadow has a sharper edge. With a bit of careful observation, you can sense the *amount* of space that exists between.

Subjective Space

A camera can show you only what is there, accurately and realistically. Our eyes are like that, too, seeing just what is there. But if we use our eyes along with our imaginations or our emotions, we can actually surpass the best camera lens in our ability to detect space. Artists can create their own spaces and manipulate them at will.

Notice the sense of space between the sheet and its shadow. The sharp contrast between white and black also helps emphasize the space. Photograph by Debra Selleck.

The light source is to the left of the jar, causing it to cast a shadow to the right. Notice the detailed definition of the lip as indicated by the shadows. Study all the jar's features as developed by the shadows. Try drawing a similar object that is located in strong light.

Space is indicated by some shadow and the curled arms of the chair, but the flat arrangement of shapes in the rest of the painting seems to defy actual depth. A tension develops, which gives the painting a dynamic quality. Juan Gris, *L'Arlequin Assis,* 1920, oil on canvas (39½" x 28"). Los Angeles County Museum of Art, Estate of David E. Bright.

Cubism and Abstractionism: Designing Space

Cubist artists—like Pablo Picasso, Juan Gris, and Georges Braque—actually redesigned the space around them. Since they believed that painting was not intended to imitate nature, the space on their canvases did not have to appear like actual space in nature. They literally created their own personal spaces in their paintings. They flattened space, fractured forms, experimented with color, added lines where none existed, and generally reshaped nature.

A cubist or abstractionist canvas can show an oblique (slanted) view of a still life on a table. But it can also allow you to see a direct profile of one vase and the top view of another at the same time in the same painting. Such treatment of space is contrary to nature and to the camera lens, but it contains the artist's imagination and creative energy.

To get an idea of this cubistic concept, take just *one* simple object—say a chair, a vase, a lamp. Do three drawings from different angles: straight on, from above, and from below. Then combine parts of the three drawings into a final drawing.

Ambiguous Space

Artists have long been intrigued with showing space that is not what it seems to be. If you look carefully around you into reflections, mirrors, distorted glass, and metal, you can also notice some ambiguous spaces. Many contemporary artists deceive the eye with line, shape, and color, causing you to question whether the space depicted is flat or dimensional. Although such optical illusions can be entertaining, they are the basis for some serious art.

A student artist has created an ambiguous shape that could be flat, could bend back in space, or both! How was this accomplished?

Transcending Time and Space

Artists, both past and present, have at times by-passed the normal presentation of space and time. In his *Transfiguration,* the High Renaissance painter Raphael painted two events happening at the same time but in two separate spaces on the earth. The early Renaissance artist Masaccio, in his *Tribute Money,* did Raphael one better: he showed three events in one painting, taking place in sequence and in different spaces. Jan Van Eyck painted his *Annunciation* as if it took place in a Gothic cathedral in about *A.D.* 1400, but the event actually took place in Israel in about 1 *B.C.*. Other artists throughout history have made similar adjustments in space and time, seeming to transcend the traditional concepts of each.

Surrealist artists attempt to create a deep space in which their illusionary subject matter exists. At first glance, their space appears true enough, but after a careful look, it often becomes extremely subjective and personal—an artistic creation having little relationship to reality. Surrealist artists conceive a "twilight zone" of space to accommodate their depictions of fantasy—a dreamlike world where objects and places are combined in ways not possible in the real world.

Other Design Projects

Cut out five circles of different sizes from one color of a sheet of construction paper. Place them randomly on a contrasting color sheet. Notice that the larger circles appear closer. Add a horizon line to the paper and place some circles above it and some below it. Notice the changes in spatial concepts. Try different arrangements. What happens?

Take a full-page photo scene (such as a cityscape or landscape) from a magazine. Cut it into equally sized squares or rectangles. Now rearrange the pieces until you are pleased with the design. Rubber cement them into their new positions. What has happened to actual space?

Use another magazine photo that shows objects in a scene that stresses deep space (perspective going into the distance). Place the imaginary vanishing point where you think it belongs. Then use a ruler and draw converging lines from any objects back to the vanishing point. This should help you when you wish to use linear perspective in your own designs.

Use your name or a different word made of large, printed letters that are drawn in the following ways: thick and blackened in; just outlined with empty space inside; outlined with edges rubbed and blurred; and textured or patterned. Place them in a row (as you would normally do) and observe the visual sense of advancing or receding space. How have these techniques affected the sense of depth?

Make a simple form using wire. It need not be a recognizable form. Try to make it interesting to view from all angles. Also, try to make the empty spaces vary in size and shape.

Do a drawing based on the wire sculpture. Use heavy outlines to represent the wire that is closer to you and thinner lines for the wire that is farther away. Then lightly shade in the empty, or negative, areas that are farther away. Let the blank paper represent the negative areas in the design that are close to you.

Cut out people from magazine photos or even snapshots. Rubber cement the cut-out people onto a background (a scene you've drawn or painted or a scene from a magazine). Then add objects that interest you but that would not be seen together in the real world. (These might also be your own creations or photo cut-outs.) Arrange these into your design without worrying about realistic perspective or proportions. You have created your own sense of space, similar in some ways to what the surrealists have done.

In this oil painting, the space is infinite—there seems to be no definite background, and sky and earth blend in a way that seems to defy ordinary space and time. The title itself and the strange forms add to the mystery. Yves Tanguy, *The Furniture of Time,* 1939. The Museum of Modern Art, New York, Collection of James Thrall Soby.

Texture is an important art element in providing visual enrichment. Dorte Christjansen's large batik hanging uses a variety of textural patterns to enhance shapes.

Texture

Just imagine what it would be like to live in a world where everything had the same surface or feel. It might be somewhat terrifying and probably unpleasant. We are lucky to have such a variety of surfaces to add to our visual environment.

One of the prime ingredients of surface quality is *texture.* Texture denotes a material's characteristic physical structure. Woven fabrics, for instance, have particular textural surfaces ranging from subtle, closely knit fibers to heavy, three-dimensional interwoven materials. The texture readily identifies the material: for example, glass is smooth and slick, and sand is gritty.

Texture can be manipulated to create artistic effects. Just as some artists or craftspeople use lines, shapes and forms, colors, values, and space, others use texture to give a particular look or feel to their work.

To understand texture's importance in our lives and in art, take some time to experience its qualities fully. Start by exploring textures in a room by touch only. With your eyes closed, let your hands diagnose objects and surfaces by the sensations delivered through touch. Group together a number of objects that have diverse textures, and analyze the ingredients that create these surfaces. The smooth slick surface of glass contrasts with the coarse feel of thick drapes or a heavy woven sweater. Notice in particular the size of the texture, the shape of the texture, and the arrangements of textures (for example, light and compact, or loose and open).

Outdoors you can encounter the wide variety of natural textures, some that are obvious, like the bark of trees, and others that are subtle, such as fine spider webs or winter frost on a window. Try jotting down quick descriptions of the textures you see outside. Next to those descriptions make a small sketch of a section of that texture. You might also collect interesting textural objects for further study or to put together in a collage.

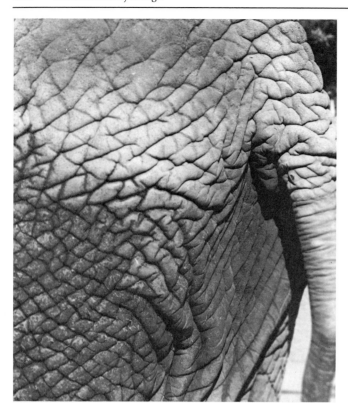

Skin texture can be smooth, lightly creased, or—as in the case of an elephant—pronounced and distinctive.

An artist selects materials that effectively portray the textural feel of subject matter. Smooth marble is an ideal medium for a snail's surfaces.

Surface Qualities

Real Textures

As viewers or as artists, we experience two kinds of textures: *real* and *implied*. Real textures are those that we actually see and touch in our environment. Implied textures are simulated or invented. Real textures have both look and feel; implied textures offer only the appearance of texture.

Since real textures were here long before anyone tried to simulate them, they are much more abundant than implied textures. The importance of real textures is that they provide us with clues about an object's nature and, to a large degree, about its function. The texture of elephant skin seems quite logical for the elephant's survival and function in rugged African or Indian terrain. A snake's slick, smooth surface allows it to slide swiftly over and through ground coverings.

Many textures have a protective purpose. Prickly plants and spiny animals give fair warning that their surfaces are unpleasant to touch. Consequently, humans or other animals avoid touching them. Many textures attract. We enjoy the soft feel of cat fur, the smooth, refreshing quality of bed sheets, or the reflective surface of polished wood.

Real or actual textures create a welcome relief to plain, unadorned areas. Architects are highly selective in using textures to modify and enrich the visual look of a building. Wood, brick, stucco, glass, and metal offer variety and contrast. Artists can manipulate paint with brushes, knives, and tools to produce texture. The paint can be applied thickly in areas so that it stands up from the surface. It may be worked with brushes and other painting implements to form actual textural patterns—the kind you can feel with your hands. We are often tempted to touch paintings that have this textural appeal to see if they feel like they look.

For textures to be appealing, their use must be controlled. Too much texture or the wrong type of texture can disturb a surface's appearance. Hence it is often necessary to use areas of refined or quiet-looking texture as visual rests from active textured areas. Raised, bumpy, pebbly, or craggy textures are visually active; low-relief, fused, and closely knit textures are more passive and restful. Using smooth against rough, heavy against light, jagged against slick produce interesting surface texture contrasts.

Texture is an integral part of an object or a form. All our experiences with texture build a memory file that we retain and re-experience when we contact implied textures. This memory bank also reinforces our judgment in appraising all manner of textured surfaces we eventually encounter. Like burning your finger on a hot stove, your memory of experience retriggers itself in similar occasions.

Abstractionist Richard Diebenkorn knows the value of paint textures to impart visual qualities. Brush strokes and thickness of paint are the principal textural ingredients. *Berkeley #24*, 1954 (68¾″ x 57″). Norton Simon Museum of Art at Pasadena, Gift of Mr. and Mrs. Robert A. Rowan.

Implied Texture

Rembrandt, Jan Vermeer, Frans Hals, and other seventeenth-century Dutch artists were highly skilled in painting surface appearances. Whether they depicted the tough feel and glisten of armor or the soft, undulating folds of silken fabrics, they knew how to show (how *to imply*) the texture of these materials. Their textures helped to describe the character of their themes and to give an air of realism. Such skill required careful observation of the surface appearances of forms and a knowledge of ways to depict those qualities graphically.

The painter has paint, brushes, and flat surfaces to use in representing textural images. Another artist may use a printing press for graphic textural qualities. One process of etching uses a soft ground agent on a plate to pick up applied textures like fabrics or wood grains that are actually pressed into the ground surface. These textures are etched into the plate in acid baths and eventually inked and printed. The resulting image of these textures relates to what we know them to be from actual experience; we see and, in a sense, feel them when we view their simulated appearance. Even in abstract or non-objective art, implied textures are important for expressive visual effects. These textures suggest certain feelings and moods, or perhaps even ambiguities. They may be an organizational device to unify areas or to repeat certain patterns.

By using implied textures, the artist has "fooled our eyes" in a sense. We are experiencing something that is not an actual reality but rather an impression of one. All implied textures that the art world offers reflect our daily experiences with textures.

Creative artists not only portray textures but also skillfully invent them to enhance their ideas. The textures of shapes, and values can heighten the intensity of artwork, and we can sense that intensity as we visually explore the creative solution.

Michelangelo's consummate skill with marble enabled him to render the "implied" textures of flesh and fabric, as exemplified by his *Pieta*. Photograph courtesy of the Italian Cultural Institute.

Using the textural feel of surfaces can be the major concern of a contemporary artist, as we see in this environmental treatment of subtle textures, composed of ceramic pieces set in sand. Connie Zehr, *Place Between Two Waters*, 1973. Courtesy of the Orlando Gallery, Encino, California.

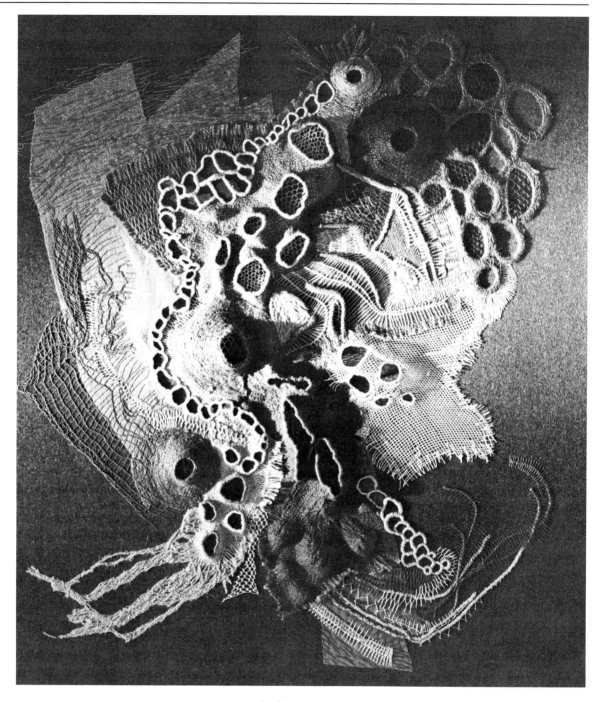

Light cast on surfaces helps to intensify the textures of materials. Evelyn Svec Ward, *Gray Morning,* stitching, cut work, appliqué (32″ x 37″). Museum of Contemporary Crafts, New York.

Light and Texture

We know that light determines how well we see all the visual elements. Once the light source diminishes, forms, colors, lines, and textures lose their identity and character. Since texture is primarily a surface quality, light has a pronounced effect on its readability. When the light is right—that is, when it is bright enough and in the right position—textures become active and dominant. Photographers know that the late afternoon is ideal for dramatic outdoor shots, for the light comes in at a low angle and casts superb shadows. When this angled light hits a textural surface, it strongly defines the heavily textured areas. Each part of the texture that is sufficiently raised casts its own shadow, thereby increasing the contrast between lit and shaded areas.

In contrast, a highly polished surface texture will bounce bright light off its surface. In the glaring surface the texture's identity is lost. The more a surface texture is kept in low relief or polished to a highly reflective surface, the more it loses definition and character under strong light.

Some materials, such as a dull satin fabric, absorb considerable amounts of light. Such textures are easily seen under normal lighting. On round surfaces there is a gradation of light moving from a high-keyed area to deep values, so textures will be strongly evident on top surfaces and lost in the deep recesses.

Just as well-placed light sources can have handsome effects in galleries and store fronts, lighting can also be an integral part of displaying textured art objects. A well-lit ceramic pot can achieve a rich textural appearance, whereas similar forms lose their significance with overpowering or poorly placed light sources. Try some experiments with light sources and textured forms to enhance surfaces. What happens with side lighting, back lighting, and top lighting? Can you also create new textural patterns by manipulating lights to cast shadows that produce textural arrangements?

In using texture in an art form such as sculpture, the artist knows how light will affect the final work. Sample pieces of textured material may be tested for their receptivity to light. This kind of critical analysis helps the artist to achieve the right results from materials. In sum, you can see that light and texture go hand in hand to make the most of rich surface qualities.

Gold, silver, and precious stones have been used in this chalice to achieve an elegant look. Textures from each of these surfaces contrast with one another. Chalice of Abbot Suger of Saint-Denis. Widener Collection, National Gallery of Art, Washington, D.C.

The textures of grass or tree bark and twigs have been richly detailed in this drawing by Vincent Van Gogh. This approach to enrichening surfaces with textures became a dominant theme in his later paintings. Courtesy of Stedelijk Museum, Amsterdam, Holland.

Texture is part of the energetic use of line in this 1947 pen-and-brush study, *Man and Horse,* by Marino Marini. Baltimore Museum of Art, Nelson and Juanita Greif Gutman Collection.

Artists and the Use of Texture

When you think of all the kinds of materials that artists use today to express idea, you will see that texture is an inherent quality in all of them. Paint, clay, fiber, wood, metal, stone, and plastics—all have distinct textural surfaces.

Paint's texture may be very obvious, as in heavy impasto oil painting, or extremely reduced, as in thin washes of water-based media. Some artists—Van Gogh and Willem de Kooning—used thick, textured applications of paint to create highly energetic forms that almost seem to leave the surface of the canvas. This type of painting makes us extremely conscious of surface levels and the ridging of paint that turn shapes into three-dimensional forms. Jackson Pollock and the school of action painters used the thickness and texture of pigments to build up rich, complex surfaces with poured and flung paint. This freely applied technique creates whole surfaces of texture that build on top of each other to produce a network of surface patterns. Texture becomes a natural product of the painting act.

In the hands of a skilled potter, clay can produce a wide variety of textured surfaces. The imprint of fingers on wheel-thrown clay forms produces a uniform textured pattern. Various tools can be used to work textures into soft and semihard ceramic pieces. Additives, like clay grog, also give clay a course, sandy surface texture. Glazes added to fired work produce a smooth, opaque, or crackled texture. Some potters deliberately throw salt into the kiln during the firing process to pit the surface of glazes and produce a texture similar to volcanic rock.

Throughout the centuries artisans, weavers, and fiber artists have produced fibers and fabrics with rich offerings of texture. Early Egyptian fabrics are still revered for their unparalleled finely woven materials. The beauty of native woven materials from Africa, the South Seas, Guatemala, and American Indians reflects the skill of these craftspeople to use patterns and textures that are unique and satisfying.

Softening the harshness of architectural surfaces is easily achieved by introducing textured materials such as these bricks seen on a detail of a contemporary building in Baltimore, Maryland. Courtesy of Meyers and D'Aleo, Inc., Architects and Planners.

This treatment of a silver sun face stresses surface texture, the result of carefully grinding and polishing metal.

Sculptors achieve textural qualities by selecting materials that give certain surface effects, or by using tools to change surfaces. Wood can be carved, gouged, sanded, or polished; each process gives a particular textural quality. Metals can also be treated to achieve significant textures through cutting, welding, brazing, grinding, and polishing. Smooth marble often produces a surface texture that achieves the striking appearance of human form, as seen in Greek and Roman sculpture or the work of Michelangelo. These sculptors could simulate the texture of skin or the soft folds of fabric. Sculptors today also explore the potentials of plastic and synthetic materials using new processes such as vacuum forming and epoxy laminations. Textures can be imbedded in plastic, and surfaces can be finely polished. Lighting is often an integral part of modern sculptural pieces.

Two-dimensional art relies heavily on implied textures, which are drawn, depicted in paint, or achieved by means of a print process. A skillful pencil drawing can portray a wide array of textures ranging from wrinkles in a face to the ripples in water.

Printmaking creates new challenges for the artist to exploit a new spectrum to textural possibilities. It may be the grain of wood in a wood cut, the etched lines in a zinc plate, or a unique grouping of adhered materials to produce a collagraph.

In your own explorations with media, you can try to imaginatively emply textures that belong to particular materials, and to produce your own invented textures. What the artist does with texture, how fabricated products manipulate it, and how we see it used in buildings, clothing, advertising, and environmental control all indicate that texture is an essential aspect of sight and touch. The textures introduced into city planning through landscaped parks, shopping malls, building exteriors and interiors, artwork, and even the surfaces we walk on strongly reinforce texture's importance in producing a pleasing visual environment.

Human beings have a strong preference for order in the visual world, and arranging the elements of design into cohesive patterns for living has been a continual effort. Shapes, forms, colors, lines, and spatial areas are controlled in building design and exterior landscaping, so texture must be carefully considered also.

Machine stitchery with natural raffia was used creatively to weave this textural landscape. Adrienne Kraut, *Landscape* (20" x 20"). Courtesy of The Museum of Contemporary Crafts, New York.

Sidewalks along city streets don't have to be long ribbons of uninterrupted surfaces. Textured cement and the texture from plants and trees can provide relief and enjoyment. Parks and landscaped area can offer a rich variety of textures from grass, shrubs, the bark of exotic trees, and walks of crushed rock or imbedded pebbles. Fences and dividers can have rich wood textures. Walls can be constructed with patterns of differing brick surfaces. Schools, churches and synagogues, municipal buildings, hotels and recreational structures often integrate texture into their designs. These textures may cover whole surfaces or just provide detail enrichment.

Our homes offer unlimited opportunities to introduce textural enrichment. The carpeting, draperies, and furniture we select can be enhanced by appropriate texture. In sum, our lives become more interesting with visual variety. Texture is an exciting element that increases the quality of design in our lives.

Other Design Projects

Once alert to the unique textures that surround us and the appeal to our sight and touch, it becomes natural to try to use texture in art-directed ways. These activities could be part of a program to put texture into action.

Using a collection of found textures (bark, leaves, seeds, pebbles, and so forth) form a design using groupings of similar textures. Try several arrangements, then glue down the best solution onto a surface such as wood or cardboard.

From a group of diverse objects, make a series of pencil or pen-and-ink renderings that capture the look and feel of those textures.

Experiment with a dry brush and paint or ink to produce the feathery look of grass, shrubs, and tree foliage. Use a wet-into-wet technique with watercolor to simulate softer textures.

See what kinds of interesting textures you can make from inking and printing both found and invented textures.

Make a sculpture from cardboard or papier mâché. Try embellishing surfaces with real and implied textures.

Cut out a number of implied textures from magazines and try to fit them into an improvised landscape.

Design a room and show with sample swatches (cloth, wallpaper, and so on) how you would introduce texture to enliven surfaces.

Pour mixed plaster into molds made with damp sand, and imbed a variety of textured objects into organized patterns. Contrast imbedded objects with textures made with various tools before the plaster has set.

From observation and touch, make two lists that contrast smooth and textured shapes.

Gather a number of intriguing textural surfaces, such as tree bark, crushed paper, or various seeds, and make a texture board by gluing areas of textured shapes to a board. These can be placed into geometric or free-flowing designs to provide an organized format.

A number of drawings can be made to closely simulate both smooth and textured surfaces. Other simulated textures might use more involved media, such as watercolor, tempera and mixed media.

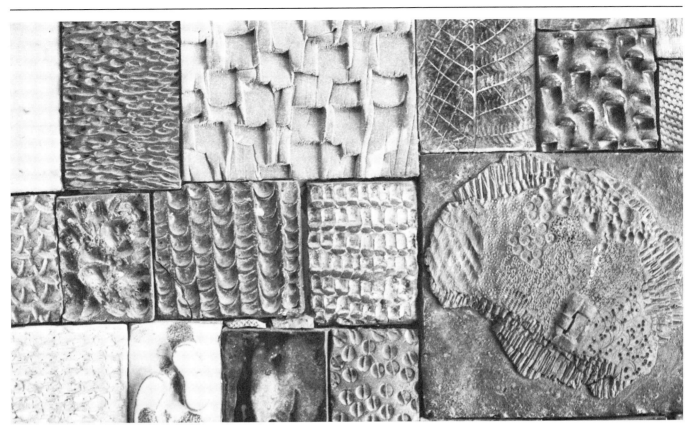

Rich textural surfaces can be made by manipulating clay with tools, fingers, and pressed-in objects. Detail, ceramic wall, Villa Park High School, California.

Innumerable textures can be made by inking and printing surfaces such as wood, fiber, or found objects.

Feathers are challenging textured objects to use for pen-and-ink studies. Santiago High School, California.

To make elements of art work effectively, artists or designers must follow certain guidelines or procedures to help them present their ideas competently. Fortunately, a number of principles have been applied to design and art, which have functioned extremely well to assist the organizing process. They are broad rules that work for increasing both visual sensitivity and creative order.

The organizing devices are balance, unity, contrast, emphasis, movement, rhythm, and pattern. They are rarely used separately, although you should examine and understand each principle. Rather, they are used in concert with each other more often. A design may use balance to achieve equilibrium (both sides equal), but it may also contrast certain areas, emphasize parts of the design, achieve rhythm and movement, and produce an overall pattern. Each principle helps to reinforce the organizing aspect of the other principle; one may dominate a design and yet be supported by minor use of the others. One important aspect of experiencing and understanding these principles is that you can gain the benefit of more sensitive vision. The designer sees the world a great deal differently than does the untrained individual.

The ability to enjoy what we see means seeing aspects of design that enhance the quality of received images. Unquestionably, top photographers have a

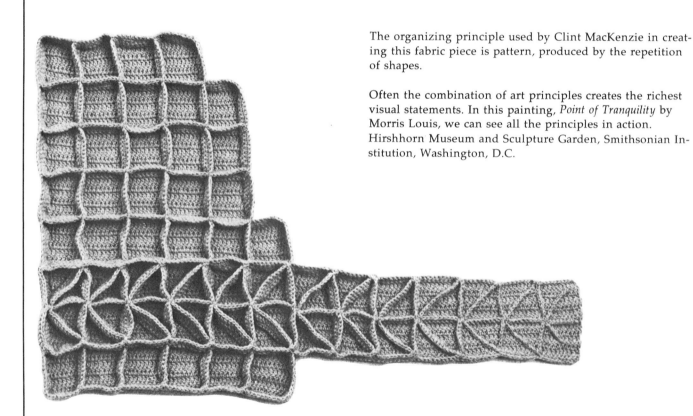

The organizing principle used by Clint MacKenzie in creating this fabric piece is pattern, produced by the repetition of shapes.

Often the combination of art principles creates the richest visual statements. In this painting, *Point of Tranquility* by Morris Louis, we can see all the principles in action. Hirshhorn Museum and Sculpture Garden, Smithsonian Institution, Washington, D.C.

Part Two

way of viewing things that focus on important visual qualities of life. We can learn to develop this kind of vision by increasing our awareness of design principles. As you study the following chapters on these ideas, test them in your everyday viewing of life around you. Instead of seeing a set of chairs as a number of miscellaneous forms, view them as a pattern of shapes or a rhythmical interplay of forms, colors, and values. Try to experience trees as moving rhythms or contrasting forms or balanced images.

When you combine your "seen" design experiences with efforts to produce design, the two activities will join and strengthen each other. Thus when you learn to see principles of design as an everyday experience, then perception will function when you draw, arrange, or compose with art media.

The art principles are used to unify or organize visual expression, and can be used in every aspect of art production. As these principles become a part of your own design knowledge, you will gain new fluency and expressiveness. Furthermore, your design skill will reflect this visual ordering and communicate itself to others, for everyone responds to order and richly composed work.

The Principles of Design

Raymond Duchamp-Villon used cubist techniques when he created the bronze sculpture *Le Grand Cheval* in 1914. The horse takes on mechanical characteristics and is asymmetrically balanced. Collection of the Walker Art Center, Minneapolis.

Balance

Have you ever walked on a railroad track, on the top of a brick wall, or on the trunk of a fallen tree? As long as you kept your balance, you felt comfortable. But if you began to lose your balance, you felt panic and an immediate need to get back into balance. One of our most important needs is to stay in balance, not only in physical balance, but in mental, psychological, and visual balance as well. Often the crying of the infant comes from its sense of a sudden loss of balance. From the earliest times in our lives, we are at odds with the forces of gravity, and we soon learn how to balance muscle pull against muscle pull, how to stand erect, and how to move about with ease.

Similarly, the artist strives for balance because it makes the work seem comfortable and at ease. Sometimes, however, an artist may wish to use balance, especially informal balance, to create tension. Balance in art is so fundamental to a unified composition that it is impossible to present the problems of design and organization without considering it.

Balance is an optical condition in art. The human brain tends to accept visual images that appear balanced and to reject images that appear unbalanced.

Several factors contribute to balance in a work of art when they are combined with the visual elements: location or placement, size, proportion, amount, and direction. There is also a need for enough harmony to create unity, but enough variety to create excitement. Of all these factors, location is the most significant. There are three types of locational balance: *symmetrical, asymmetrical,* and *radial.*

Symmetrical Balance

Of the three kinds of locational balance, symmetrical (or "formal") balance is the easiest to understand. It is the simplest way to achieve balance, but it can also be the least interesting way. Symmetrical balance occurs when the objects on each side of an imaginary center line are identical. Think of yourself balanced with your feet side by side, on a narrow board or rock, with both arms extended to the side. You are in symmetrical balance. If one arm is dropped or raised, you will become unbalanced, and begin to lean to one side.

Look in a mirror and notice that your face is *almost* symmetrically balanced. A well-shaped fir tree is sym-

metrically balanced, as is a well-shaped apple. Artwork that is exactly the same on both sides of an imaginary center line is symmetrically balanced. One side is the mirror image of the other side. It is easy to recognize symmetrical balance if the composition is simple and has very few parts, but sometimes the visual elements may seem complex and difficult to understand. But as soon as you recognize that both sides of the picture plane are identical—and that the picture has symmetrical balance—you will experience a sense of ease and satisfaction.

You might experience symmetrical balance by making several "channel prints." Fold a piece of heavy drawing paper in half, and rub the crease to make a sharp fold. Open it again and drip various colors of tempera paint and/or ink in the center. While it is still wet, refold the sheet and press from the crease to the outer edges, spreading the colors inside. When opened again, your channel print should be symmetrically balanced because you have created a mirror image.

Because of its identical repetition, the effect of pure symmetrical balance is usually static, so viewers can lose interest quickly. Some artists may actually wish to establish a feeling of monotony or non-excitement in their work.

If you have two identical forms on the picture plane, they will balance at any points equally distant from the center. Try using two pieces of colored paper that are equal in size, color, value, and shape. Place these on a larger piece of white rectangular paper. Move the two shapes away from an imaginary center line, observing the balance that occurs. Examine what happens when the shapes are moved to the extreme edge of the white paper, and what happens when the shapes are moved very close to the center. After you have explored many locations, you can paste the shapes down to form a symmetrically balanced collage. You may wish to add other shapes to make a more complicated design, still keeping the composition symmetrically balanced.

This church interior design is identical on both sides of the center. The lines, forms, and textures are symmetrical and convey moods of strength and durability. First Presbyterian Church, Stamford, Connecticut.

This photograph of a butterfly allows you to see one example of symmetrical design found in nature. Can you think of others? Photograph courtesy of Eastman Kodak.

An example of a channel print, which exemplifies symmetrical design and balance.

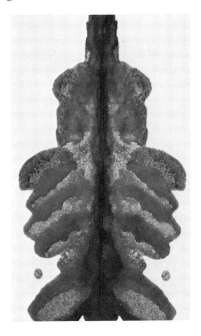

An imaginary line drawn down the center of this hand-carved door would illustrate symmetrical balance.

This poster, part of a safety campaign, is symmetrically balanced. Identical shapes mirror each other on both sides of the center line. Courtesy of the Automobile Club of Southern California.

Barkley L. Hendricks used symmetrical balance in establishing a quiet mood for his painting *Miss Johnson*. Photograph courtesy of School Arts Magazine.

Approximate Symmetry

Some artists have tried to break the severe monotony of pure symmetry on the pictorial surface by a method that is sometimes called *approximate symmetry*. The two sides of the picture plane are varied enough to hold the viewer's attention, but they are similar enough to make the repetitious relationships of symmetrical balance evident.

Asymmetrical Balance

Asymmetrical balance (or "informal" balance) is more complex and interesting than, yet equally as satisfying as, symmetrical balance. Asymmetrical balance often contrasts elements through a *sensed* equilibrium between parts of a picture. For example, it might be achieved between a small area of strong color and a large, empty space on the pictorial surface. Or a very bright, small area of color might balance a large, dull one. Since asymmetrical balance is sensed and not actually seen, there are no rules for achieving it in a painting or drawing.

Asymmetrical balance is interesting because of the unlimited possibilities and combinations it offers. However, it is more difficult to achieve and understand than symmetrical balance. There is no center line—real or imaginary—and no dividing axis. Even if there is a dividing line, one side of the design will be different from the other side.

You can experience actual asymmetrical balance by making a small teeter-totter. Balance a wooden ruler or flat piece of wood on a fulcrum (balance point) of some sort (a pencil, a triangular block, or other raised ridge). Place various objects on each side of the center and move them until they are balanced. A small, heavy object will balance a large, light object. Some objects will have to be moved closer or farther from the fulcrum to achieve balance. Even though the objects have various weights, sizes, and shapes, you can balance them in an informal way.

When Alexander Calder and other twentieth-century artists created mobiles that moved in air currents, they were making use of asymmetrical balance. You might like to develop a mobile that can be suspended from above. If you do, begin with the bottom elements in the design and work toward the top. That

Despite the vast amount of visual activity on this Japanese woodblock print, close observation reveals an almost perfect form of symmetrical balance. Utagawa Kuniyoshi, *Actor*. Collection of Joseph A. Gatto.

The large, dark area at the right is balanced by a small, dark-valued shape surrounded by light values. Alexander Nepote tried several locations for the small shape but felt it was most comfortable here, creating asymmetrical balance. *On the Beach, Alone* is a watercolor and collage work.

Vincent Van Gogh used the size, color, and position of the bed as he balanced this painting asymmetrically. The negative space of the floor, the table chairs, and the dark value of the window create visual balance. *The Artist's Bedroom at Arles*, 1889 (72" x 90"). Stedelijk Museum, Amsterdam.

The designer of this poster placed the lettering, logo, and artwork to produce an asymmetrical design. The light-valued areas are dominant and need to be carefully positioned to achieve balance and unity. Courtesy of the Automobile Club of Southern California.

way, each part of the mobile becomes a problem in asymmetrical design and balance.

Two-dimensional art (drawing, painting, and print-making) needs balance to make it look comfortable. Informal balance can provide that feeling of comfort and yet still produce a sense of excitement and interest.

As you manipulate the visual elements, you can sense, judge, or estimate the opposing forces and their tensions so that they balance each other in total concept. Working with the visual elements is an instantaneous form of communication: you do not have to wait for the results of your ideas. Through your intuition, you will soon discover the amount of a particular element to use: how much bright against dull, large against small, light versus dark, geometric versus organic.

Use several of these combinations to create informal, visually balanced designs. Cut or tear shapes from papers of various textures, colors, and/or values, and place two of them on a sheet of white paper. Using two contrasting sizes and colors, see if you can position them to create a feeling of balance. Try a small piece with intense color and a large piece with dull color. Use a small, textured piece with a larger, smooth piece of similar color and value. When the results *feel* comfortable, you have probably achieved asymmetrical balance.

Look at paintings and sculpture throughout this book to see how artists and designers have achieved asymmetrical balance in their work.

The small, dark-valued boats, surrounded by sand and sky (light values) balance the composition of *Beach in Normandy* by Gustave Courbet. If you cover the two little boat shapes with gray paper, you will see how important they are in establishing a feeling of balance. National Gallery of Art, Washington, D.C., the Chester Dale Collection.

Rose Window, Notre Dame (1194-1220). Photograph courtesy of the French Government Tourist Office.

Radial Balance

Radial balance radiates from a central point. An example of radial balance is the bicycle wheel, which has a central axle and spokes radiating out to a perfectly round rim and tire.

Designs based on radial balance relate somewhat to formal balance in that they are generally static, orderly, and quiet, and in that they create a feeling of stability and security. The principal difference is that the various elements contained in this type of design are arranged in a radiating sequence around a central point, forming a circular pattern.

Rose windows—found in many churches in the United States and in almost all European cathedrals—are excellent examples of radial balance used in architecture. In fact, these round windows were first called "wheel windows" because they resembled wheels. An example of this use is the Rose Window from the Cathedral of Notre Dame in Chartres, France.

Interesting variations of radial balance can be created by altering the number, direction, and spatial arrangement of the parts of a design. In spite of such modifications, radial design tends to demand repetition, which creates an overall decorative effect.

What natural objects in your environment have radial balance? Many flowers do, as well as some vegetables and fruits if they are sliced in half. You might want to make a list of such things in nature that would contain radial design, or even prepare a display of such items. A camera might help you share your finds with your classmates.

Can you think of things that are manufactured or created by hand that might have radial balance? Wheels, gears, dials, lamp shades, and manhole covers are some. Can you list others?

A print, made by inking a paper doilie, is an example of radial balance.

Radial balance is evident in the core of this chambered nautilus. The entire photograph, with its light and dark contrasting values, is an example of asymmetrical design and balance. Photograph courtesy of Eastman Kodak.

Max Bill's granite sculpture is balanced physically and visually, and has a symmetrical appearance. It appears to be balanced on a very small point, but it is actually anchored into the base.

Other Design Projects

Use cut papers, cardboard, and/or cloth scraps to decorate a mask. You can make the mask itself from heavy paper, cardboard or papier mâché. Try to keep the features in symmetrical balance, but still try to make the work colorful and exciting.

From a piece of red, yellow, or orange paper, cut out one large and one small shape. Do the same with a piece of blue, green, or violet paper. Arrange these shapes on a piece of white paper. Which shapes have heavier visual weight? Can you balance a small, warm shape with a large, cool shape?

Select some texture samples (cloth, fibers, metal, sandpaper, and similar surfaces). Place them on a piece of paper and attempt to visually balance coarse textures with smooth ones. What adjustments must you make in the size of the shapes to achieve visual balance?

Fold a piece of paper in half and use scissors or a stencil knife to cut a design. (You may draw the design first or cut without any drawing.) Keep the fold as part of the design. Then open and flatten the design and paste it to a paper of contrasting color and value. Is your design symmetrical or asymmetrical?

Set up a still life in the classroom. Attempt to arrange similar objects on both sides of a central form for an example of symmetrical balance. Make drawings of the still life, attempting to maintain the concept of symmetrical balance.

Select photographs from magazine sources that illustrate symmetrical, asymmetrical, and radial balance.

Analyze numbers and alphabet letters to determine which are symmetrical and which are asymmetrical. Perhaps you can use this information in a design or a chart.

Make a painting in which you attempt to create balance by contrasting the art elements. Contrast warm and cool colors. light and dark values, smooth and rough textures, large and small shapes.

Cut out some landscape elements—such as trees, mountains, hills, fences, barns, animals, and shrubs—from colored construction paper or from magazine pages. Try several arrangements of these pieces on a sheet of paper, taking care to achieve visual balance. When you are satisfied, glue them in place to finish your collage.

Artists who use abstract shapes and ideas must be careful to position the elements of their work to achieve balance. Pauline Eaton, in *Central Valley,* used collage and acrylic paint but balanced color, texture, and value carefully.

Unity

All of us have heard the football coach or principal talk about team unity or school spirit. Both coaches and school administrators realize that a group of people can produce a much better result if there is unity among them—if they are all working toward a common goal or purpose.

Think of the unity involved with a team of sled dogs or the unity on a tug of war team. The need for such unity is evident when we realize that without it, the dogs would run in different directions and the tug of war team would not be pulling together.

Artists of all kinds are concerned with similar problems. They want their work to have a unified feeling: a sense of completeness and harmony. They want all the parts of their creations—paintings, drawings, pottery, architecture—to work together to produce the best possible result. A ceramist wants the decoration to match the feeling and proportions of the pot's form. An architect wants the parts of buildings to belong together visually.

The opposite of unity is disunity, which usually implies chaos and ruin. For a work of art to feel complete and finished, a sense of unity must prevail. Disunity will produce a sense of disorder and implies that the artist was unskilled.

A team of superstars often cannot beat a team that has played together for many years. Even though the superstars are all great athletes, if they don't give up a little of their personal glory for the team, they can't unite for victory. In the same way, a work of art may have some super parts, but if the artist does not take care to unify them, the result will not be complete or unified. It will not present a finished appearance.

Dominance and Subordination

A painting will probably have unity if a *single* strong element or particular subject dominates the painting, and if other elements or subjects are used to support the main subject.

A painting may have one design element that dominates all the others. An impasto painting may have an overall textural quality that will unify the surface. A drawing may be mostly made up of lines, or a collage may be made from cut shapes. A single color might seem to run through an entire painting, creating a certain mood and unifying the various parts. A strong sense of perspective might unify various parts

Winslow Homer used many techniques to develop unity in *The Carnival.* He distributed various values and colors throughout the painting; he used a single strong light source; the central three figures act as a single strong unit, dominating the scene; there is strong repetition of vertical shapes and lines; he skillfully used asymmetrical balance; there is a carefully contrived eye movement leading to the center of interest area, where the sewing is going on; and finally, there is a visual story (narrative) involving the carnival performers (who are repairing their costumes) and happy children. The Metropolitan Museum of Art, Lararus Fund.

A huge tree assumes a dominant position in this painting by Andrew Wyeth. The rest of the landscape features are subordinated. The distribution of contrasting values, visual weight, and the central location of the main subject matter aid in unifying the composition. *Cider Apples,* 1962 (18¾″ x 24″). Los Angeles County Museum of Art, gift of Maurine Church Coburn.

A single, strong figure produces an obvious dominant shape on the picture plane. But line is a dominant art element, with value and color subordinate. Both these qualities produce unity in Torii Kiyonobu's woodcut *Woman Dancer*, 1708. Collection of the Metropolitan Museum of Art, Harris Brisbane Dick Fund.

of a painting or drawing. A painting of all dark values or all light values will be unified because of the similar value pattern over most of the surface. In each case, if a single design element is dominant and others are subordinate, the picture plane will have a unified and harmonious surface.

Some paintings and many sculptures are single-unit structures, having only one major subject, shape, or form. Because this unit is so obviously alone, it is practically all we see and therefore is unified. If there were several strongly competing units, there may not be such obvious unity.

From magazines, cut out several advertisements for automobiles that show one automobile in a dominant position. Perhaps there will also be a dominant color. Try to explain how all other features are subordinate to the dominant automobile and color.

Repetition of Visual Units

Perhaps you have noticed that some buildings seem more unified than others or that some neighborhoods have a similar look. In doing so, you were responding to the repetition of certain visual units. For example, rectangles and squares may be repeated over the surface of a high-rise structure. A neighborhood might have similarily shaped houses or streets lined with elm trees. Can you think of items that could produce visual unity in a neighborhood? Can you think of things that make neighborhoods look unharmonious?

Artists can use repeated units to develop a feeling of unity: repeated circles, arcs, rectangles, triangles, or squares; or repeated vertical, horizontal, or oblique lines or shapes. A color can be repeated in several parts of a painting. Certain knots can be repeated in a macrame design, and patterns of colors can be repeated in a weaving.

The single, column-like form dominates this Northwest Indian sculpture, while the individually carved forms are subordinated. This 23-inch sculpture is carved from wood, with abalone shell inlaid for color and reflection. The single strong form makes a unified appearance. The Hauberg Collection; Whatcom Museum of History and Art, Bellingham, Washington.

A structure such as Moshe Safdie's *Habitat '67* in Montreal could become visually chaotic. Overall unity is established, however, by the repetition of cubelike forms, all of which relate to each other. Photograph courtesy of Moshe Safdie and Associates.

Sieg der Sloop „Maria"

Lyonel Feininger's watercolor is unified because of repeated shapes (rectangles and triangles), repeated colors and values, and repeated lines. *Victory of the Sloop, Maria,* 1925 (10⅝" x 16⅞"). Los Angeles County Museum of Art, gift of Dr. Phillip Rothman and Edward Rothman.

Burgoyne Diller's carefully designed painting avoids monotony because of the variety of widths in the lines and the variety of sizes and shapes of the spaces that are formed. *Second Theme,* 1937–1938 (30⅛" x 30"). The Metropolitan Museum of Art, George A. Hearn Fund.

Kerry Strand programmed a computer to create this linear design. Although the computer plotter made individual lines from one side of the design to the other, the combination is visually unified because repeated shapes were created. A central focus is also established. Courtesy of California Computer Corporation.

Too much repetition of a single feature can produce monotony, so artists are careful to add some variety to their work. They might repeat a shape but give it a slightly different color. Or a color may be repeated with a slightly different shape. Circles may be repeated but with different sizes, or some might not be completed. If added carefully, such variety will increase interest and yet will not endanger the unity of the composition. A well designed building may be unified with a repetition of rectangular shapes and forms, but varying the sizes or shapes or colors of the rectangles will prevent monotony.

Piet Mondrian and Burgoyne Diller designed paintings composed of thick vertical and horizontal lines and several rectangular spaces. Such a painting is certainly unified, but it might seem monotonous at first glance. Careful study will show, however, that in many cases, the thick lines have slightly different widths and the white rectangles have slightly different dimensions.

LeRoy Neiman used cool colors as the dominant hues to unify this serigraph (silkscreen print). Spots of warm color, the center of interest area, form a contrast. Courtesy of the artist.

Robert E. Wood used analogous colors in this watercolor. Can you determine the colors that he used? Lighter values in watercolor are made by thinning the washes with more water to make them more transparent. Darker values have a dark blue color added, because Wood does not like to use black in his work. Courtesy of the artist.

Use of Color

If you make a painting by covering an entire canvas or paper with a flat coat or a single color, you have certainly created a unified surface, for color is an important element in developing unity. But you can easily see that such a painting might be very monotonous. If you use the same color of blue to paint trees, houses, people, birds, flowers, grass, and sky, you will not be able to distinguish one part from another. If you add varying amounts of white and black to the color, you can make tints and shades of the color and thus be able to distinguish the various objects in the painting. The painting will still be unified because the color blue is common to all the values present.

You can also use analogous colors (other colors containing blue in their mixtures) and still retain a strong feeling of unity because blue is still present in blue-green and blue-violet, or even in green and violet. Try painting a landscape, still life, or geometric design, using a single color, plus one or two other colors containing that single color in their mixtures. For example, use red as the main color, and add red-orange and red-violet. You may also wish to include orange and violet. These five colors can be intermixed without endangering the unity because they all contain red. Even if you were to change the values by adding black and white, the unity will still persist.

If such a design or painting seems monotonous in its color, you could add small amounts of a complementary color to the center of interest. How else could you introduce variety and not hinder the unity?

Often you select clothes on the basis of "what goes together." This is simply another way of saying that you want your clothes to project a sense of unity and harmony. Select several magazine advertisements that show clothing and discuss how the designer used color to achieve unity and still produced enough variety to make the design interesting.

Paul Cézanne often used a dominant color in his paintings. He liked to call it the "mood color." Even if he used every color of the spectrum, he would mix a bit of his mood color into each to give the entire painting an overall feeling of unity and harmony.

The freely brushed strokes in John Constable's oil painting help unite the elements of sky, cathedral, trees, and foreground. *A View of Salisbury Cathedral,* (28¾″ x 36″). National Gallery of Art, Washington, D. C., Andrew Mellon Collection.

Thickly applied, brusque brush strokes are used throughout this Van Gogh painting. Such strokes unify the surface but writhing lines add contrast and prevent monotony. *The Olive Orchard* (28¾″ x 36¼″). National Gallery of Art, Washington, D. C., Chester Dale Collection.

Surface Quality

Sculptors, painters, architects, and craftspeople are often concerned with the surface quality of their work, because texture can help develop a feeling of unity. If the textures of various parts of a building, bowl, sculpture, or woven fabric seem to work well together, the unity of the product will be strengthened.

Some painters work with similar brush strokes in all parts of their work to unify the surface. Some strokes, like those of Auguste Renoir, are soft and rather long. Others are jabbed onto the surface and are thick, like those of Van Gogh. Cézanne's brush strokes seem square and almost chiseled. Some can be liquid, wide, thin, or transparent. Some painters use painting knives, which produce a characteristic surface quality in which the paint seems to be buttered onto the canvas.

A sculptor may wish to unify a work by developing a textural surface that has similar characteristics in its various parts: fingerprints, scratches, tool marks, projections, indentations, or a smooth quality.

To keep all such textured surfaces from becoming monotonous, artists may change textures slightly, use various colors or values, or change shapes. They may also change the sizes and shapes of items in the painting to keep the total work from becoming too much the same.

You might try making a simple drawing, painting, print, or ceramic piece in which the entire surface is united with a similar textural feeling. Try using your fingertip and an ink pad for your medium. Or try using all vertical lines to make a pencil drawing. Use only one type of brush to make a painting and allow the brush strokes to show—that is, don't smooth them out. Make a ceramic sculpture and texture the entire surface in a similar way.

Such design problems will make you aware of unified surface qualities. Generally, you should introduce some variety in the textures to sustain interest and avoid monotony.

The surface of Vincent Van Gogh's *View from Vincent's Room* is covered with dots of color. Even though this textural quality unites the painting, the artist added several areas of contrast and variety. Can you locate them? Stedelijk Museum, Amsterdam.

Jan Hoowij has developed a unique and personal style of
painting landscapes. In *Doors of Perception II,* he is telling us
that there is more than one way to look at mountains. Technique and style work together to produce harmony and
unity. Courtesy of the artist.

The Artist's Style

An artist's style or technique can also contribute to unity in a work. If artists are consistent in the way they use style and technique, their work will have a characteristic feeling that may lead to unity. However, style alone does not assure unity.

Paintings may have hard edges between colors and shapes. If this pattern is consistent throughout the painting, it can assist in the creation of unity. All the objects, including the background, may have a flattened look, or a rounded look. All the brush strokes may show, or perhaps none of them may show. An abstract expressionist painting usually includes slashing brush strokes throughout the work.

An artist's techniques, such as airbrush, collage, wet-into-wet washes, or impasto can also help achieve unity. A stylized treatment of subject matter, if used consistently in the painting, will help too. Unity might also be developed by emphasizing the large shapes, softening the edges, outlining everything with a heavy dark line, or using any other technique that tends to create noticeable similarities on all parts of the surface.

Special care must be taken when working in various mixed media combinations. Often such combinations can become chaotic, because the excitement of unplanned "happy accidents" can lead to an unharmonious surface. In such cases, other techniques for achieving unity might be used (distribution of colors, repetition of visual elements) to keep the surface unified.

The linear quality of the work plus the characteristic feeling of an etched metal plate work together to give unity to Joan Miró's etching, *Young Girl Skipping Rope, Women, Birds,* 1947 (11¹³/₁₆″ x 8¹⁵/₁₆″). Collection, The Museum of Modern Art, New York, Purchase Fund.

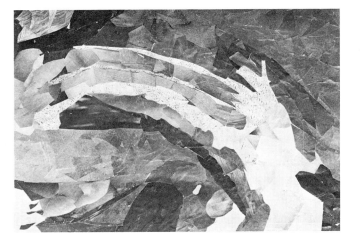

When all the parts of a collage are cut and have crisp edges, the entire surface has a feeling of belonging together, even though colors, values, and textures are different. Lutheran High School, Los Angeles.

Pencil or pen can be used to shade a still life (or other subject matter) with only vertical lines, developing a strong sense of unity and harmony. John Marshall High School, Los Angeles.

The entire surface of this student design is covered with colored wool yarn. Such a single technique and application creates a harmonious surface. Wilmington Junior High School, California.

Other Design Projects

Make a pinch pot out of clay and apply an overall pattern with a single tool—such as a fork, a piece of bark, or a nail—while pressing into the soft clay.

Create a painting using one color and tints or shades of that color to produce a unified work.

Set up a still life arrangement. Try to cluster the forms close together to unify the arrangement. Draw several views of the set-up, attempting to stress unity by closeness and clustering.

Make a design based on converging or radiating lines. (Unity is possible because the eye moves to one point along the lines.)

Draw a floor plan of a room or a house. Try to arrange furniture and accessories in the drawing to create dominant and subordinate elements.

Make a painting with analogous colors. You may wish to introduce black and white to make tints and shades.

Make a collage of a subject of your choice, using small, rectangular paper shapes cut from magazines. Unity will be achieved through the overall pattern of similarly shaped and sized pieces. A mosaic look should be the result.

Make a pencil drawing by first sketching the objects in a still life. If you do all the shading by using vertical lines, you will produce a very unified feeling.

Cut out interesting photographs from magazine sources. Select one photograph that is more interesting than the others, using it as a center of interest. Place the other cut-outs around and near the center of interest, attempting to create unity by central location.

A unified feeling is expressed when all the parts of a collage have similarly torn edges. How else did the artist strengthen the feeling of unity?

Scratches made with wooden tools are repeated around this ceramic bell. The character of the decoration seems consistent with the texture and form of the bell.

Contrast

Our lives are filled with contrast of all kinds. We have emotional contrasts: we feel joy at a wedding and sadness when we see illness or helplessness. We see contrasts in nature: the dramatic stripes of a zebra, the bright features of a male bird. We see contrasts in our cities and towns: old houses being torn down and new buildings going up. After eating a hamburger, you might have a dish of ice cream, not necessarily because you're still hungry, but partly because of the pleasurable contrast of the taste.

Many other contrasts affect our lives and help shape our personalities. We all need variety in the things we see and do. Artists, film-makers, musicians, authors, and dancers use contrasts in their work to add variety, change the pace, or develop or emphasize a mood. We will use the term variety to describe small differences and the term *contrasts* to describe larger differences.

Artists may be directly influenced by contrasts, whether the subtle variety of the different greens in a forest, or more dramatic like the light and shadow patterns of early morning. Even abstract or non-objective art can be influenced (perhaps subconsciously) by contrasts that exist in the real world. The force, and even anger, of a powerful brush stroke may be the extension of one painter's concern for humanity. Another painter might be more interested in the brush stroke itself as the paint contrasts with another color or with the white canvas.

Natural and Man-Made Contrasts

When prehistoric people lived in caves and dug out areas in which to sleep and cook food, the relationship between nature and people-made designs began. This and the following examples of the partnership between natural and man-made objects demonstrate contrasting elements working together.

Perhaps you see someone arrange a bouquet of fresh flowers, put them in a man-made vase, and place them on a window ledge where a natural background of trees and sky blends as part of the composition. Or you look out the window at a telephone pole standing next to a tree. The wires from the pole reach toward the tree branches, intermingling in an interesting pattern.

Most of us gather objects around us to have handy to use or
to enjoy their look, their touch, or the memories they bring
us: books, plants, old photos, rocks—many contrasting
things.

An excellent example of the relationship of natural and man-made things can be seen in the Anasazi Indian dwellings in Arizona's Canyon de Chelly. The natural rock formations provided protection from intruders and the weather.

David Smith's geometric and abstract sculpture contrasts beautifully with the natural, large pine trees in the background.

Artists paint natural scenes and also use natural materials to make their designs. Sometimes these natural materials describe something else—a piece of driftwood may represent the wing of a bird, for example. In another design, however, the wood may remain just a piece of wood. A finished work of art may be placed in a natural setting, such as a sculpture in a garden, which is yet another example of the partnership of natural and man-made objects.

Kinds of Contrasts

There are many kinds of visual and psychological contrasts, from subtle to bold, both in art and in nature. In this section, we will mainly discuss bolder contrasts that include big to small, dark to light, straight to curved, geometric to organic, rough to smooth, warm to cool, many to few, shallow to deep. Such contrasts may also be used to convey a mood of joy, sorrow, fear, and indifference.

Artists use the contrasting qualities of the art elements—line, color and value, texture, shape and form—in their work for a variety of reasons. They may wish to delight our eyes, set a mood, establish a rhythm, or make some visual statement that grabs our attention or even spurs us to action (perhaps in a poster design).

Certainly there can be many different kinds of contrast within a single piece of artwork, but to understand the roles that the art elements can play, we will discuss them singly.

Line Contrasts

Thick, bold lines create a strong effect. When they are contrasted with delicate lines, they can affect the sense of space in a design. The bold lines may appear closer if there is no overlapping. If the delicate lines *do* overlap the bold lines, space may seem to exist between them. If the lines are similar in length and direction and close together but still separate, they may create a strong optical illusion or visual vibration.

Georges Grosz contrasted varied line thicknesses, broken and flowing lines, and brushed-in ink areas to add vitality and a sense of urgency to this drawing. Note the gestures and expressions of the figures. *Street Scene*, 1931/32, black ink and white brush drawing (18½″ x 23¼″), Los Angeles County Museum of Art, Mr. and Mrs. William Preston Harrison Collection.

Shape and Form Contrasts

Shape and form contrasts offer the artist many opportunities. Similar shapes of different sizes also create space. The larger shape will generally advance visually, or it may seem to be more stationary because of its *visual* weight. The smaller form may seem to have the freedom to move about because of its *lesser* visual weight. A smaller, more organic shape may visually balance a larger, simpler shape. Even though the organic shape is smaller, its complexity attracts our attention and gives it visual strength. Angled or sharp-edged shapes can be very dramatic, but they may need to be balanced with some curved shapes to make a composition more interesting.

Many contrasting forms can be seen in this African sculpture. The face is round until it tapers to a point at the chin. The eyes are angled shapes, and the shells that decorate the top of the head have their own interesting form.

Texture Contrasts

Texture contrasts usually are used to bring visual interest to the design or to strengthen the artist's personal message or idea. If a completely smooth surface seems boring, the artist might "rough up" an area to change the pace. To show the horror of war, for example, an artist may contrast rough, textured areas with smooth areas—perhaps the rugged battlefield and barbed wire will contrast with smooth human flesh. Rough, thick strokes of paint could contrast with delicate, thin washes in an abstract way to suggest the conflicts of battle.

Heavily textured surfaces also tend to advance visually. It is important to remember that a design may have only *one* texture and still be interesting. A Van Gogh painting, for example, has thickly applied paint throughout, but *other* contrasts exist through the use of line and color.

Bold, angled dark and light forms contrast with each other and with the circular shape of the canvas. Rinaldo Paluzzi, *Spatial Construction.* Courtesy of Silvan Simone Gallery, Los Angeles.

Notice the skillful handling of the different textural surfaces—the coat fabric, the collar, the shirt, and the face in
this oil and acrylic painting by Barkley L. Hendricks.

Color Contrasts

Color contrasts present many exciting possibilities for an artist. Warm colors may be placed next to cool colors. Bold, vibrant colors may be juxtaposed with soft, muted ones. When complementary colors are put side by side, they create very powerful contrasts because our eyes naturally seek out the opposite color. You can test this yourself: Place a bright red circle on a green background, then gaze at it steadily for a few minutes. Afterward, when you look away at a blank wall or ceiling, the colors should reverse so that a green circle appears on a red background.

Colors are used in many contrasting ways in this painting. Some are applied loosely and quickly, some fuzzily, and others crisply and boldly. Compare the color of the green headscarf and skin on the face in the upper left with the graffiti on the cars. Colleen Browning, *Pep's Car with an Assist from Clyde, Snake and Peabody,* 1975. Courtesy of Kennedy Galleries, Inc., New York, Collection of Letty Pogrebin.

In another painting by Hendricks, very bold colors in the clothing contrast with the bright red background. Notice how the red in the clothing, by being similar to the red in the background, sets up a visual vibration. *Blood,* 1975, oil and acrylic (72″ x 50″).

Henri Matisse used color in many ways in this oil painting to evoke the mood of a pleasant day. Some colors are dulled in shaded areas, while others are applied bright and clean. The colors were also brushed on in a variety of ways: short, quick strokes contrast with smoother, large areas of paint. *Tea,* Collection of The Los Angeles County Museum of Art, Bequest of David L. Loew.

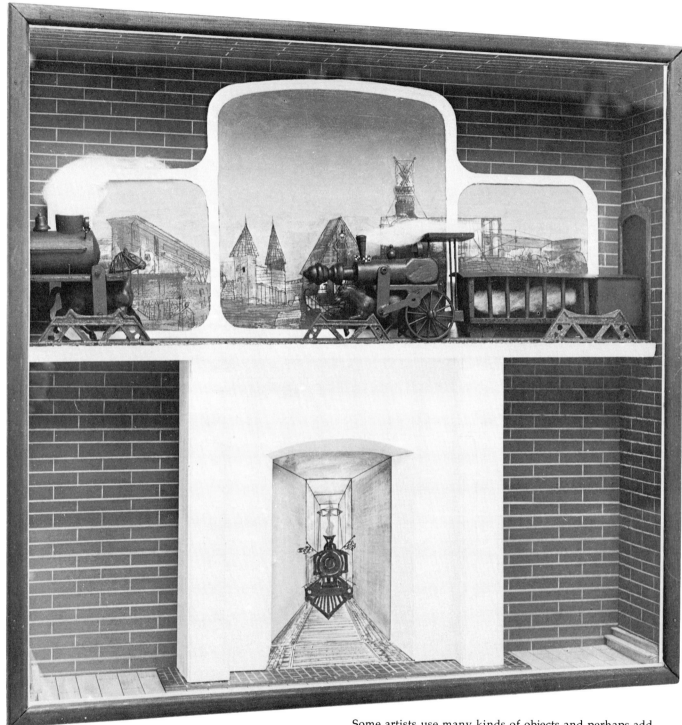

Some artists use many kinds of objects and perhaps add their own drawing, painting, and imaginative combinations to produce assemblages or constructions. This one is by Gordon Wagner. Note the three-dimensional trains with puffs of "cotton smoke." The lower train is a painting.

Contrast in Materials

Many artists use one medium or material to create their particular designs, whether they are painting, constructing, printing, or sculpting. Some artists, however, use more than a single material. There are some built-in advantages in doing this—different textures, colors, and values are automatically available. The mood or feel of the work can be expressed quickly, and the visual and tactile possibilities are endless.

These materials can be gathered from anywhere and used for many different kinds of designs. A furniture designer may combine metal, fabric, and wood to create a chair. An architect may combine many materials—stone, metal, wood, glass, plastics, and natural plants—whether designing a single-family house or a large building complex. In the art classroom, you can combine simple materials such as paint and sand (for texture) or balsa wood and fabric in a three-dimensional design.

You may want to try a project made from scrap or found objects. Try to vary the textures and shapes and coordinate the colors. There are two basic ways to approach this project: (1) Think of what you want to make and then gather the necessary materials, or (2) gather the materials first and let them "tell" you what to make.

Broken records, tin, leatherette, a sprayer, and other odds and ends were incorporated in this motorcycle assemblage mounted on wood.

An artist must know how to use dark and light in order to work in a representational manner. John Singer Sargent (attributed), *Portrait of a Man*, c. 1900, oil on canvas (30″ x 24″). Los Angeles County Museum of Art, Mira T. Hershey Memorial Collection.

In this hard-edged painting, rectangles of various sizes and values create a visual shifting of space. John D. McLaughlin, *Untitled*, 1955, oil on masonite (38″ x 32″). Los Angeles County Museum of Art, Los Angeles County Funds.

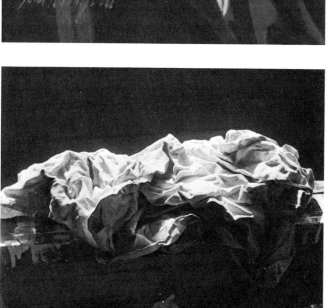

A paint rag, dirty and stiff from dried paint, is transformed into a dramatic, beautiful form as sunlight plays on its folded and wrinkled surface.

Contrast Among Like Things

There can be variety and contrast among like things. People, for example, or apples, or flowers. Something as simple as a trip to the store can become a visual adventure. Similarly shaped items, when displayed with care, can present patterns of colorful and tactile pleasure. Designers can choose one subject or motif (which gives them a definite beginning) and then, by varying it, create an interesting work of art.

For variety, the artist might use size contrast, or perhaps stages of growth—young and new, or middle age, to old. Using different techniques can also vary the object. For example, a design using horses for subject matter could depict some horses blurred to suggest movement, others rendered carefully to emphasize types, and some simplified with flat shapes.

Pick one object or subject, and by using any of the contrasts mentioned, try to create a design of "like things."

Contrast—Dark and Light

Exciting examples of light and shadow contrasts are all around us. As you get dressed with the early morning light spreading into your room, glance out the window and see the beauty of light and shadow on the trees. As you ride in a car, you can see the variety and differences of the light and dark inside the car, contrasting with that outside. If you walk under a pier in the late afternoon, you can see the play of light and shadow creating fascinating patterns on the sand and pylons. A figure sleeps on a bus bench. The light and shadows that cross his face and clothing dramatize the restful form. You leave the movie theater through the rear exit into the alley, where fuzzy lights and dark shadows tease the imagination. You find yourself dashing to the brighter lights and activities on the main street.

Whether working naturalistically or abstractly, artists have been interested in the effects of dark and light and their dramatic possibilities for hundreds of years. The contrast between dark and light can be used to create strong designs, frightening moods, dramatically modeled forms, and a sense of space or environment.

Many materials are available for experimenting with dark and light contrasts—charcoal, india ink, heavy crayon or pencil. Some artists use materials beyond these basic ones—neon, fluorescent, and incandescent light, and even laser beams.

Dark and light may be created by natural sunlight or by artificial light. Some artists may draw or paint scenes where they suggest natural or artificial light in their designs. A sense of light and dark can exist as a representation of actual light and shadow. Or the artist may use colors, values, and forms that evoke a sense of light and dark without particular reference to real things or real sources of light.

Take a large black-and-white photograph of a face from a magazine. With a brush and india ink, go over the dark and medium dark tones in the photo. Then use white poster paint to cover the light areas. This sharp reduction of natural light to simplified white and black areas should dramatize the extreme contrast of dark and light.

Though some type of contrast exists in most scenes or art-works, there is often a stronger contrast that exists in the mind. In this drawing, a single object is located in an empty area, but the crucial contrast is the floating book and its shadow. This depiction defies the way we normally see a book. Edward Ruscha, *Suspended Book,* 1970, gunpowder and pastel on paper, drawing (11½" x 29"). Los Angeles County Museum of Art, gift of Contemporary Art Council.

Many contrasts exist in this wall painting—color, shapes, values, and light. But it is the strange image of buildings reaching into space, seemingly through other buildings, that plays on the mind.

An ordinary object such as a comb, when seen as a giant work of art, sets up a contrast that is fascinating and difficult to ignore. Vija Celmins, *Comb,* enamel on wood. Permission to photograph from Los Angeles County Museum of Art.

Contrast in the Mind

Though some type of contrast exists in most scenes or artworks, there is often a stronger contrast that exists in the mind. When we contrast things, we are also making comparisons. Comparison is the identification of similar, or like, characteristics. It is obvious that when we look at any work of art—whether it is realistic, abstract, or non-objective—we relate it to our own existence, our likes, dislikes, past experiences, and knowledge. For example, if you look at a realistic 30-inch x 40-inch painting of a landscape, it may conjure up memories of a similar scene that you've actually observed, and you can easily understand and accept the artist's interpretation.

Should another artist present a landscape with simple, vertical strokes representing trees and splotches

of green as leaves, we need to understand what feeling or visual intent the artist had. In other words, our mind relates his or her version to our ordinary idea of trees and leaves.

If another artist has trees floating serenely through the sky along with the clouds, our mind contrasts this even further with trees and clouds as we know them. Artists, then, may use styles or techniques that dislocate us momentarily and put us into their world. Our mind must make the contrast with the real world and begin to deal with the artwork on its terms.

Compositional Space and Balance

Some artists and photographers are interested in the sense of space offered by nature or by the materials they use. As mentioned in the last chapter, symmetrical balance (equal shapes, forms, or objects on both sides of a central line in a design) has some advantages and disadvantages. This type of design is very formal, strong, and solid. A fern leaf with a central stalk is a good example.

As you know, the disadvantage of symmetry is that in certain cases it can become visually boring. The artist may alleviate this boredom by changing color, texture, and value so that the two sides of the design, though still structurally strong, are more interesting visually.

Try this yourself. Divide a piece of paper in half. Then draw large, identical shapes (perhaps two circles), one in each half at the same location. Add two more shapes of a different kind inside the first two. Now add a third inside the second two shapes, identically located in each half of the design. The design should have a strong, simple, symmetrical balance. Then, by using color, texture, and/or value, make the shapes different in each half of the design. You have probably eliminated the visual monotony of the original design.

Many artists avoid this concern by making asymmetrical designs. In these designs, a bright-colored, small shape may balance a larger, more dully colored shape. A long, thin, wiggly line may be interesting enough to visually balance a heavy, angular shape. A complex shape or textured form may balance a large, brightly colored form.

Time and Motion

A work of art, such as a mobile or a motor-driven sculpture, can actually move or it can appear to move through the use of certain techniques such as angles, directions, and color sensations. Sometimes, as the viewer moves, the artwork appears to move. Time can also be a factor in our viewing.

You walk along a city street and see a new building located near an old one. The span of years stands before your eyes as you compare the different architecture of the two buildings. And your knowledge of or actual participation in that time span offers a fascinating contrast between past and present. A field may be plowed, but the curving furrows remain as a reminder of the action that took place. Sitting on a hillside, you notice a field of flowers, some just buds eager to open, some fully grown and stretching towards the sun, and some already wilted. A composite of time is within your momentary view.

Photographer/artist Michael Stone uses photographs taken from television and then seals them in plastic containers. The result has a haunting effect, as if these images have been packaged for future study.

These two photographs are of the same moving sculpture—in one the circle is closed, and in the other it is set in motion and the circle is "broken." A sense of time is conveyed because of the cycle that will return the sculpture to its original shape. Jerome Kirk, *Broken Circle* (56″ high).

Other Design Projects

Cut out an organic shape from colored construction paper. Then cut out a triangular shape. Place them on a neutrally colored sheet. How does the contrast between the two shapes affect the sense of space? The sense of movement? Is there a mood involved? Why?

Using india ink and brush, place a small, circular shape about the size of a quarter near the upper left corner. Brush in a large, bold, angled shape in the central area. Then place a squiggly, long line running from the lower center up toward the right central area. What effects do these contrasting shapes have concerning direction, movement, and balance?

Make an animal form out of clay. Smooth the surface completely, then add texture to some areas of the design. Does the texture add a visual interest to your design or does it seem unnecessary? Now try varied textures on the whole animal. How do they affect your basic idea? Do they change the character of the animal? Which of the three versions do you prefer? Why?

Use photos of yourself or a family member or friend that cover the years from infancy to the present. Try drawing from them, not being overly concerned that the drawings look like the person, but concentrating instead on the youthful to older appearance. Then try a combination drawing in which parts of three faces and/or bodies are coordinated into just *one* face and/or full body view. You have created a composite of time based on contrast.

Look carefully at a reproduction of a famous painting (preferably in color). Jot down the different contrasts that you see *or* sense. Consider the art elements as well as psychological concepts.

Using the same painting, zoom in on a section (perhaps using a paper view-finder) until you locate an area that by itself could be a well-designed, non-objective painting. What contrasts exist in this small section? Do they give you ideas for a larger version that could include your own additions?

If you have a camera, scout around school or home to find examples of interesting contrasts. You might concentrate on size, color, texture, dark and light, and so on.

To help you discover exciting, new ways of balance and composition through contrast, start a "busy scene" painting or collage. Place a shape or object that you would ordinarily locate in the central area of your design in a corner of your paper or canvas. Let this challenging position help you complete the design.

Much contrast is shown in this student's work. Shapes are of many kinds and sizes, dark and light areas are strongly contrasted, and many materials were used, including paint, collage, and pen and ink.

A photographer must compose the photograph in the camera lens. Emphasis here is on the small U.S. flag in the window. A large area of relatively little visual activity allows our eyes to settle on the smaller area of strong value contrasts and heightened visual activity. A knowledge of how emphasis can be achieved allowed this photographer to arrange the subject carefully to carry the message.

Emphasis

At this moment, what do you consider the most important and significant aspects in your life? Did you feel the same way last year? Three months ago? Yesterday? Throughout your life, you are confronted with ever-changing ideas, situations and moods, some of which are more important than others. You sort them out, identify them, and assign them different sets of values. They either retain their importance, gain in stature, or lose their emphasis in your life.

In our society, we place great importance on the individual. Significantly, only you can determine what should be emphasized in your environment and how much you will allow outside influences to change your life. Emphasis is a personal point of view, because what may seem very important to you could be rather insignificant to others. And each of us tends to surround ourselves with art, objects, and material that seem important to us.

Just as you stress these significant aspects in your life, so does the artist, who is influenced by the same forces, tensions, anxieties, moods, and ideas as the rest of us. However, artists must also sort out, evaluate, and establish priorities in their work, and determine just how they will express these priorities to their audiences.

Emphasis is not a difficult principle to understand. You need only listen to music, look at art, or read literature to realize that composers, artists, and authors each have ways of developing a main idea, theme, or center of interest. Emphasis is developing a way of expressing your main ideas in each work you produce, each painting you make, or each sculpture you carve or construct. We develop emphasis in response to the question: "What are you trying to say in the artwork you are producing?" Let's look at some of the ways you can answer that question in your artwork.

Emphasis and the Art Elements

A viewer focuses on the different parts of a design in order of their emphasis, or importance. Part of your experience in art has been, and will continue to be, the exploration and manipulation of the art elements: line, color, value, shape and form, space, and texture. When all the elements work together to produce emphasis, a sense of harmony and unity is achieved. These principles of unity and emphasis almost always work hand in hand.

The emphasis in Paul Cézanne's painting, *Mount Saint Victory* (1904-1906), is on the technique and the painterly quality of the surface. He accomplished this by covering the entire canvas with brush strokes of the same size and allowed them all to remain visible. Philadelphia Museum of Art Collection, George W. Elkins Collection.

Unlike other disciplines, art has no prescribed rules or formulas for using the visual elements. To develop emphasis, the artist experiments and uses the art elements many times, attempting to relate them to each other and to the work. Very soon, the artist develops an affinity for one or more elements and emphasizes it in his or her work. To get an idea of this, look through this book and other art books, and list different artists whose works emphasize certain art elements. Not all artists emphasize these elements to the exclusion of the others, but some do. Piet Mondrian and Jackson Pollock emphasize line; Stuart Davis emphasized shape; Vincent Van Gogh emphasized texture; Ellsworth Kelly emphasizes shape and color. Can you find more artists to add to this list?

Emphasis may involve the inventive and expressive stress or accentuation of the art elements. Emphasis also helps organize and design a work of art through dominance and subordination, as the artist attempts to control the viewing sequence in a particular work. Try experimenting with and manipulating art media and materials—traditional or experimental—and observe what happens with the art elements. Which do you find yourself using at this time? Do you like to invent colors or create exciting lines? Is texture more exciting to you, or do you find shape or form dominating your work? Do you see a tendency evolving in your preference for one element over another? Can you make a drawing where line is emphasized, or one where value is emphasized?

As you explore a wide variety of art materials and media, you will discover that a significant variation in the elements of art is possible. A similar variation exists in nature. Select several natural forms, such as shells, bark, leaves, and rocks. Observe the wide variation of the art elements found in one natural form. Subtle variations of color, line, form, value, and texture are evident, but usually one element seems to dominate. If you were drawing or painting that form, you might also cause that same element to dominate your visual presentation of it.

Kaethe Kollwitz, like other citizens of Europe, was influenced by tragic wartime experiences during war time. She emphasized her feelings in a poster-like lithograph titled *Never Again War*. Courtesy of Galerie St. Etienne, New York.

The dominant aspect of Pre-Columbian sculpture is the simplification of form. Detail is subordinated, leading to an emphasis on the larger forms themselves. *The Jam Session* (6½" high), from Nayarit, West Mexico. Los Angeles County Museum of Art, Collection of Proctor Stafford.

This student sculpture of liquid aluminum and wire has a design that does not detract from the emphasis on line.

Emphasis through Simplicity

The eye and mind do not usually see a haphazard or chaotic arrangement of the art elements. Our minds tend to appreciate visual order in design and in the relationships of one element to the others. Emphasis is the design principle by which the eye is carried not only to the most important element in any design, but to other details in the order of their importance.

In the visual arts, several factors should be considered, such as what to emphasize, how to achieve emphasis, how much to emphasize, and where to place the emphasis. Interestingly, emphasis can be achieved by simplicity. Simplicity of the visual elements almost always contributes to emphasis, allowing us to quickly see the artist's idea or point. We need only look at Japanese and Greek art to see how emphasis can be achieved through simplicity of design.

One way to achieve simplicity is to understand emphasis: that there should be only one outstanding idea or art element in a design, and that all others should be subordinated. Are you becoming aware that simplicity and emphasis can be present in the same work? You have often heard the terms domination and subordination in design and art classes. The next time you walk down a city street, look around and determine which building or structure dominates the skyline. Further examination shows you that one of the art elements dominates on that structure. You might make a list of visually dominant structures in your town, and then make a list of the dominant elements on each structure. Can you apply this same idea of simplicity and emphasis to a rural environment, using trees, barns, and fields? Can you even apply it to the area in which you live?

Emphasis by Placement or Grouping of Objects

In Western culture, we read from left to right. If you understand the significance of eye movement from left to right in your artwork (in Oriental cultures it is the exact opposite) you will understand how emphasis through placement is possible. When you read a headline in a newspaper, you will find the story that accompanies it underneath and to the right. You will also find the more expensive and important advertisements on the right-hand pages of magazines and newspapers. The placement or grouping of subject

The elimination of most detail simplifies the subject matter and allows us to immediately be aware of the artist's emphasis and intent. Here we are to share a look at the beauty and arrangement in nature. People are unimportant and are de-emphasized. Japanese silk painting, collection of Joseph A. Gatto.

matter on the right-hand side of the picture surface tends to emphasize that area of the composition.

The concept of the ideal location for placement of subject matter was passed down by Classical Greek sculptors and designers and medieval and Renaissance architects and painters. Basically, along with the right-hand side of the composition, three other areas can be ideal. All four positions call for the placement away from the exact center, to the right or left side and above or below the middle of the picture plane (see diagram). By placing the center of interest in or near one of these preferred locations, you will produce a composition that must be asymmetrically balanced. Such positioning will also avoid a central location, which produces a "bullseye" effect that can be so visually dominant that a viewer will ignore all other parts of the design.

Placement of subject matter in ancient times was often expressed in mathematical terms, to establish pleasant picture proportions, to fix the position of the horizon, and to divide the composition into aesthetic proportions. The ideal placement was often called *golden section*, or the *mean*.

Emphasis is also possible when many forms are grouped together. The forms are seen as one form because of their nearness to each other. Forms that are grouped together tend to visually attract, rather than repel, each other because there is an immediate and intense interaction. The closer the forms are to each other, the stronger their attraction.

Barbara Weldon used overlapping layers of tinted rice paper to build up abstract collage shapes in this untitled work. Notice the location of the center of interest. Also notice that the center of interest is determined by the area of greatest value contrast (darkest dark and lightest light).

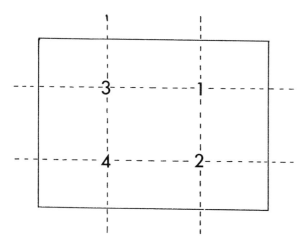

In this mixed-media drawing by Boardman Robinson, the emphasis is on the group of figures on horseback (not on individuals) located to the right of center. *Return from Moscow*, pen and ink, crayon, and tempera on paper (14⅝" x 20¾"). The Metropolitan Museum of Art, New York, gift of the artist friends of Boardman Robinson.

This large oil painting by Georges Seurat is made completely of tiny dots of color. The artist used the difficult pointillist technique, but the emphasis is still on the design itself. The center of interest is the group of two large figures to the right. There are other groupings of figures, carefully placed throughout the painting. Emphasis is on the foreground, where values and colors are more intense. Notice Seurat's use of light shapes against dark and dark against light. Also notice the repetition of several shapes throughout the work. Although large and full of figures, the painting is carefully designed. *Sunday Afternoon on the Island of La Grande Jatte,* 1886 (81″ x 120⅜″). Courtesy of the Art Institute of Chicago, Helen Birch Bartlett Memorial Collection.

Light values dominate Claude Monet's painting, whereas dark values dominate Corot's work. Can you determine how contrasting values are used in the center of interest areas? Monet, *Argenteuil*, c. 1872 (19⅞″ x 25⅝″), National Gallery of Art, Washington, D.C., Ailsa Mellon Bruce Collection. Corot, *Forest of Fontainebleau*, National Gallery of Art, Washington, D.C., Chester Dale Collection.

Emphasis through Value and Color Contrasts

Contrasting values and/or colors will also create emphasis. Your eye is attracted by strong contrasts of light and dark, because the amount of light reflected from the surface causes a strong reaction in the receptors of the eye.

Look at the work of Rembrandt to see the use of contrasting values to create dramatic light and dark emphasis. Contemporary photographers use the potential of light to create compositions that emphasize value contrasts. Observe how television, movies, and advertising capitalize on the mood and drama created by emphasized value contrasts. While value contrasts are used throughout a painting or drawing or print, the area of greatest contrast (lightest light next to the darkest dark) is often the center of interest. The artist can control this easily.

Larger areas of either strong light or dark values will dominate the rest of the picture surface. An arrangement that shows equal amounts of light and dark might be confusing. You will notice that when dark values are emphasized, they often create moods of gloom, mystery, drama, or menace. A composition with predominantly light values tends to produce opposite effects.

The use of contrasting colors is another way to achieve emphasis. The farther apart colors are on the color wheel, the more contrast our eyes record. Complementary hues provide the most contrast. Analogous colors are closely related and will not produce much contrast, unless neutrals (white and black) are added to create differing values. You might make a design or painting that uses three analogous colors throughout. You can establish a center of interest (emphasis) easily by using a complementary color in the right area, thus forming a dramatic color contrast.

Often artists and designers use both value and color to produce greater contrasts and achieve maximum emphasis. For example, light orange and dark blue will contrast more than equal values of the same color. The greater the contrast, the greater the emphasis.

In *Ali-Foreman Fight*, LeRoy Neiman used color contrasts (orange against blue, dark red against light blue, warm colors against cool colors) to emphasize maximum excitement and action. The center of interest area is emphasized with larger figures, maximum contrasts of color and value, and an off-center location. Courtesy of the artist, collection of James Knuckle.

Fritz Scholder placed his Indian figure in front of a flat red plane, thereby emphasizing the figure. Vibrant colors also place added emphasis on the subject. *American Portrait with One Eye*, 1976. Courtesy of Cordier and Ekstrom, New York.

Emphasis by Subordination of Backgrounds

On a two-dimensional picture surface, you will notice that emphasis is more effective when the background is less evident or less important than the main subject matter. An interesting thing happens when you step back a few paces from your artwork. You will be in a better position to see if there is sufficient contrast of the visual elements, between foreground and background, to create a clear visual statement. At the same time, if you squint your eyes and look at your work, the contrast of values will become more evident. Then, if necessary, you can make changes and emphasize certain art elements for greater clarity.

A simple exercise is to cut out photographs from magazines and glue or paste them onto simplified backgrounds, cut either from other magazine photographs or from plain paper. Observe how, with a simplified background, you can emphasize the subject matter. You can make comparisons by repeating this exercise, placing the cut-out photographs on chaotic or confused backgrounds of equal color and value intensity. Make certain you retreat a few steps when you view these exercises. Notice how forms gain importance when separated from adjacent forms and when given sufficient plain, uncluttered, or contrasting space for a background.

Emphasis by Isolation of Subject Matter

Closely related to emphasis achieved by a simplified background is emphasis achieved by the isolation of the main subject on the picture plane. Such emphasis can be achieved through exaggerated contrast of visual elements (such as a complex subject against a flat background) and/or the strategic location of the dominant compositional element. In some cases, such as photographic compositions, portraits or advertisements, attention is called to the subject matter by placing it against an absolutely plain background. Some early portrait painters also chose not to place their subject in any kind of environment, choosing instead to emphasize facial features while avoiding problems caused by conflicting backgrounds.

Sculpture is also concerned with location. Since sculpture is to be seen "in the round" (from many different viewing points), emphasis by isolation is important. Although the background must be considered, some sculpture is created so no supporting environments are required to achieve dominance. Greater emphasis can be achieved with a rather plain background or with no background at all.

Often, sculpture is placed against the sky or the plain surface of a building. In this way, sculptures will be emphasized much more than if they are viewed against a busy city street or a confusing background of trees and bushes.

By manipulating *f*-stops and lens openings, photographers can make backgrounds blur and fade away. This places emphasis on the main subject, which is in sharp focus. What other methods of emphasis has this photographer used to draw attention to the apples?

The old buildings in *Moved on to Goldfield* by Chuck Winter are easy to pick out because they are emphasized by their placement against a simplified background. Value, texture, and color are used to develop this strong contrast.

The Jaguar's design emphasizes beauty and function, but the photographer emphasizes the total automobile by contrasting it with the background. Texture, value, and shape contrasts strengthen the photographer's concept, along with the visual subordination of the background. Photograph courtesy of British Leyland Motors.

Emphasis through the Unusual or Unexpected

Emphasis can be created by interrupting or disturbing our normal frame of reference. Basically, we desire order in our lives, which is directly related to the rhythmic orders in nature (setting sun, seasons, heartbeats). One explanation for emphasis through the unusual or unexpected is that the human brain accepts and rejects visual images based on the degree of order or disorder presented, the degree of satisfaction or dissatisfaction, the degree of comfort or discomfort.

Often surrealistic work is carefully painted and extremely realistic, except that the overall images and relationships are disturbing, strange, and unexpected. Because of these unreal images, the artist can emphasize feelings, emotions, and ideas even though they may be difficult to comprehend.

Distorting, or stretching and changing proportions, is another way to achieve emphasis because of the importance given to unusual forms. The distorted images seen in carnival mirrors or some irregular windows are fascinating although strange. Some artists emphasize their painted or sculpted figures by elongated distortion or stretching. Others distort textures, colors, or other design elements to emphasize their visual messages.

Caricatures are drawings that tend to emphasize one or more distinguishing features of a subject. Distorting through visual exaggeration emphasizes certain traits or characteristics. A strong chin is made overly strong; a large, pointed nose is exaggerated; a dachshund's length is stretched; large eyes are further enlarged.

Emphasis by Size, Proportion, Repetition, and Number

Another way to produce emphasis is to increase the proportion of one element to another. When there is more light value than dark, more rough areas than smooth, more curved shapes than straight, more reddish brush strokes than yellow, emphasis is conveyed. The relationship or proportion of the visual elements should be obvious, with sufficient contrast to add emphasis. For example, if you want to emphasize the texture of a ceramic pot, then the texture should dominate other elements. But it should not conflict with the pot's form or color. In other words, you should

René Magritte painted with careful detail, but something strange is always seen or felt. Surrealism often uses representational images, but in strange contexts. *The Liberator,* 1947, oil on canvas (39″ x 31″). Los Angeles County Museum of Art, gift of William Copley.

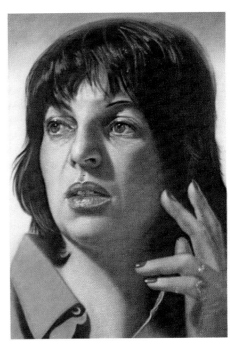

Tremendous visual impact is felt when viewing one of Audrey Flack's huge portraits. The artist is standing by her *Self-Portrait*, the same work that is shown in color. The emphasis by size is experienced only when actually confronting the painting in a room.

stress the proportion of texture to the other elements so that unity is achieved.

Emphasis is also achieved when there are sufficient numbers to demonstrate an abundance or repetition of elements. When many forms appear on a picture plane or in a three-dimensional sculpture, emphasis is achieved because the brain enjoys reinforced concepts. The idea of a crowded beach is emphasized more when dozens of human forms are bunched together than when only five or six figures are used. The concept of a jungle or dense forest is more impressive when many trees are depicted, rather than a few. Generally speaking, the more repetition of color, form, shape, or subject, the more emphasis is placed on that item in the work.

Size is also used to stress emphasis. If other factors (intensity, value, and texture) are about equal, the largest forms will be emphasized. Can you find examples in magazine advertisements where graphic designers emphasized their produce by making it larger and more important than all other aspects in the presentation?

Converging lines and shapes direct your eye to the center of interest, not only in paintings but also in nature.

Perspective lines in this photograph are unrelenting in their power to draw your eye to the point of emphasis, the box car on the track.

Emphasis by Eye Movement and Converging Lines

Artists and designers emphasize certain parts of their work by a center of interest. They can do so by using lines, shapes, colors, the edges of objects, values, or other paths along which the viewer's eye will travel. This technique is called *visual movement*. See Chapter 12 for a complete discussion of movement.

Artists capitalize on these visual movements to direct the viewer through their compositions. The area where your eye seems to land (where the movement seems to stop) is the center of interest, the emphasized part of the work. Emphasis and movement, like most of the other elements and principles of design, work together to create a total artistic statement.

Lines have the potential to create eye movement, especially converging lines. Should you decide to place an art element or subject at the terminal point of converging lines, you would give emphasis to that part of the design. In fact, the eye finds it difficult to avoid such a meeting place.

Other Design Projects

Select photographs from magazine sources (or your own photographs) that emphasize each of the elements of design: line, color, value, shape and form, space, and texture.

Design a texture board, using rubbings made with the sides of wax crayons. Arrange the samples so they emphasize the contrast between rough and smooth textures.

Using a single strand of wire, construct a three-dimensional wire sculpture. When done, draw the same sculpture in two-dimensional line. Or arrange a screen and bright light (such as a slide projector light) to have a shadow show of these wire sculptures. All parts of this project emphasize line.

Construct a collage, using natural and/or recycled materials, emphasizing textural qualities.

Select five packages from commonly used products. Discuss the art elements emphasized in each design and determine how effective the design is in selling the product. Would you have other suggestions if you were the graphic designer in charge of the product?

Make a still life set-up of man-made forms: for example, auto parts, bottles, old machinery, electronic parts. Make another set-up of natural forms: branches, fruit, leaves, flowers, and so on. Observe both set-ups carefully, and draw them, using contour lines. How do man-made and natural forms differ? How could you emphasize each quality in a drawing?

With a stopwatch or other timer, watch television programs to see how much time the commercials take. Is this a form of emphasis? In a single commercial, count how many times a product's name is mentioned. This is emphasis by repetition and numbers. Perhaps you can chart your findings and design a presentation to show the results.

Cut several strips of paper in various lengths. Lay them out on a contrasting background and arrange them to lead your eye to a center of interest. Locate this point in a desired position on the sheet and emphasize it by having two of the lines intersect. After several arrangements, glue the lines in place.

Take a series of photographs of things in your environment, either natural or people-made, that emphasize one or more of the elements or principles of design. This one emphasizes visual movement, texture, and contrast.

Pattern

The term *pattern* can be used to describe a wide variety of visual experiences and human activities. There are paper patterns utilized by the garment industry for assembling clothing; flight patterns of aircraft that prescribe the movements of each plane that lands at a busy airport; behavior patterns that indicate how people consistently react to certain life situations; or test patterns on television that help us adjust our sets for a clearer picture.

When we hear the word *pattern* in visual or art terms, we think of decorative design or the use of repeated units. We see this application of the consistent repetition of elements in clothing design, wallpaper coverings, jewelry and ornaments, architectural surfaces, and on all kinds of natural objects such as plants and animals.

Pattern uses all the elements of art. We can see lineal patterns in overhead telephone wires, dark and light or value patterns on sunlit rocks, color patterns in flower gardens, shape patterns in marching bands, textural patterns on the trunks of trees, and spatial patterns in long views of landscape and cloud-filled skies. For the artist and designer, pattern is an exciting characteristic of the forms of art, as well as the products we buy (which are richer looking). Plain, uninteresting surfaces can be vitalized with captivating patterns that delight the eye. Paintings often capitalize on the attractive qualities of pattern to reinforce shapes and surfaces. The vigorous patterns of brush strokes enhanced the work of the French Impressionists, who strove to capture the qualities of sunlight on form. Craftspeople freely use patterns to give visual beauty to forms in clay, metal, fiber, wood, and glass.

Seeing Pattern

Try exploring both indoor and outdoor environments to find the many patterns that enrich a variety of surfaces and forms. Look for the more obvious broad, large patterns, such as on the sides of buildings with windows and brick arrangements. Then look more intensely for small and delicate patterns that are intriguing forms in themselves, like spider webs, frost patterns on windows, printed circuits in machinery, or the tracery pattern on the leaves of plants. Note how pattern provides different visual sensations that help identify forms easily and interest us with their

Pattern can be free-flowing or compact. A cluster of cactus plants shows areas of closely knit patterns caused by the repetition of similar shapes, textures, and design elements.

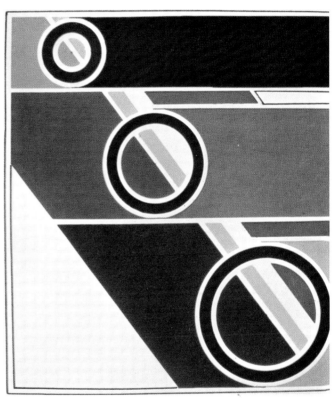

Experiments with bands of color or value will open up numerous pattern arrangements. California State University, Fullerton.

Patterns can be worn or created. This La Habra High School (California) student is manipulating paper to build optical patterns. His shirt also is patterned.

rich surface appearances. In seeing pattern, you will discover that it has two main functions: it helps to organize or unify an area or object, and it provides visual enrichment and enjoyment.

Planned Pattern

Most patterns we see are precisely planned, whether produced by people or by nature. Planned pattern involves the careful consideration of the placement of shapes or lines, values, colors, and textures so that a cohesive design is achieved. This arranging process stresses the appropriate selection of materials, the sensitive use of space, and the repetition of elements with interesting variety. Usually it follows a consistent design movement or rhythm.

You follow a type of planned pattern when you select your clothing. By choosing the appropriate patterns in shirts, blouses, skirts, or trousers, you can seem more elegant, bold, sophisticated, or even mysterious. Large, strong, colorful patterns command attention. Subtle, muted, and closely knit patterns produce a more reserved or refined effect. Often a small use of planned pattern contrasted against plain areas provides the right amount of enrichment and visual interest. Patterns of similar sized motifs may clash with each other. If used, care must be exercised to achieve a desired effect.

Planned patterns require thought and skill. The artist or designer usually will try out many approaches to pattern before finally selecting the ones he or she thinks are the most appropriate. (And if a form or shape has a distinctive enough character of its own, no additional enrichment is needed.) Even brick walls can be made more appealing by the use of planned patterns: certain brick sizes, spacing, placements, or textural surfaces. Architecture abounds in planned patterns, as is evident in banks of windows or ribbons of concrete that adorn the facades of buildings.

Nature is a master designer of pattern. Its pattern is purposeful, usually produced to camouflage a species, or to assist a bird or animal in attracting members of

An architectural designer carefully selected and arranged the brick patterns in this municipal courtyard. Note the variety of brick groupings to achieve interest.

Random patterns are unplanned arrangements of similar motifs such as these shoe prints in the sand. Shape, textured soles, and indented surfaces are the principal ingredients.

its own kind. We can easily identify many animals or birds just by the patterns we see: a leopard's spots, a tiger's stripes, or a peacock's plumage. Nature's patterns have been a rich resource for designers and art students. Many of the planned patterns we see in plants or on animals seem appropriate to use directly, such as in collages, mosaics or weavings. It is also interesting to ink their surfaces and print their patterns on paper. See if in your own discoveries of natural pattern there are some that would be intriguing to use for an art project, either directly or to achieve a patterned design by a print process.

Random Pattern

Random means by chance or without purpose. Many patterns just happen, caused by accidental arrangements or produced without any conscious design considerations. This often occurs when we spill or spatter a colored liquid onto a surface. Random patterns are usually asymmetrical (not identical on both sides), irregular in their elements, and non-uniform. These conditions can make random patterns expressive and visually exciting. The lack of planning creates an energetic look to pattern design. Action painters capitalize on the power of freely applied paint that creates striking random patterns.

A walk along a beach will often reveal many random patterns of footprints that were accidentally formed as people's paths criss-crossed. Aging wall surfaces are good places to discover random patterns: the effects of weathering wood, peeling paint, or graffitti. Random patterns are interesting to see for their unique qualities, spontaneous shapes, irregular spacing, textural changes, and overall impact.

As you view patterns in your own environment, note how often you see a mixture of random and planned pattern. Try making pattern designs where both types are used, such as carefully drawn and spaced line arrangements contrasted to a page of flipped-on paint or ink.

Tar drips on a wall surface created a strong random pattern of black shapes and lines. Also evident is a more muted pattern of cement gravel shapes and textures.

The motif is the arrowhead; the pattern is formed by repeating the motif in radiating ellipses.

After repeating a shape to form a pattern, further embellishment with line and dark areas will enhance the overall visual impact. Santiago High School, California.

Basic Patterns

Motifs and Repeats

Each pattern we see has a basic element, or *motif*, that is repeated to produce the pattern. Motifs are like the basic themes in music that reoccur to unify the work. A motif may be simply a dot, a line, or a square. Or it may be a very complex shape with intricate textures and areas of color or value.

Motifs can be placed in numerous ways, horizontally and vertically in lines or bands or staggered as in half-drop and alternating designs. They may also be in curved or radiating directions, in gridlike formations, or along rhythmical paths. The simplest pattern is achieved by repeating the same motif along one line or along several similar lines. We frequently observe this kind of pattern in the shelves of supermarkets where similar products are grouped for convenience, such as rows of soda bottles or milk cartons. Plowed fields are simple line-repeat patterns. A referee at a football game wears a line pattern on his shirt.

Look for intriguing objects, both natural and manmade, to use as printable motifs. You may wish to design your own motif and produce patterns that are variations of placements of elements. Even on a line of motifs, different groupings and spacing will give added interest. Also explore reversing the motif to produce mirror-image patterns. Single motifs could also be grouped to form a larger complex motif, and then repeated with space between to start a large-unit repeat pattern. Another interesting approach is to dissect a motif into segments, and to use both the whole motif and parts to form patterns.

Designing motifs and using them for repeated patterns is an excellent way to understand the processes of pattern development. From this basic procedure you can move onto the challenge of a more diversified use of motifs.

Grids

One of the easiest patterns to discern is the grid. Grids or networks are formed by intersecting vertical and horizontal lines or shapes that are usually uniformly spaced. If you were to mark out a series of points one inch apart both vertically and horizontally, and then draw lines through those points, you would

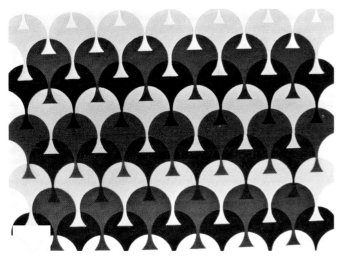

Attractive patterns can be developed from repeated motifs, and enriched with color and value. California State University, Fullerton.

form a grid. The grid could be a simple lineal pattern in itself. Better still, it could be a basis for developing a pattern by using shapes (motifs), colors, textures, or a combination of these elements in a regularly repeated fashion.

We see grid patterns in a variety of uses—gridirons or football fields with regularly spaced lineal units to mark off the yards, checkerboards, automobile grills, waffle irons, honeycombs, and the grids formed by city streets intersecting each other. Most of our contemporary architecture utilizes the grid structure. Some forms, like Fuller's geodesic dome, are pure forms of grids curved into hemispheres to create coverings for usable space. Many painters and designers use the grid as a basic structure for their work. Piet Mondrian used a flat, gridlike format in many of his major works to insert color and value patterns in paints. Weavers produce fabrics from looms where grids of warps and wefts establish the underlying foundation for woven pieces.

Grids provide equal emphasis throughout the area enclosed. Although we think of grids as being arranged up and down they could be diagonal or circular. They may be various shapes, as long as the overall effect is precise and uniform.

One grid pattern superimposed on another will often create a vibrating optical effect. These patterns, called *moiré* patterns, add an exciting visual dimension to the simple grid.

After trying some simple grid patterns with line using straight, vertical, horizontal, or diagonal lines, explore overlapping patterns, alternating patterns on grids, and composites of several grid patterns. Also try building three-dimensional grids from paper, cardboard, or balsa wood.

You will find that grids give a strong structural quality to pattern. Although they are basically simple, grids can become extremely complex when you compact the network, overlay several grid patterns, or use diverse colors, textures, and values.

Architects often utilize an alternating pattern to achieve visual interest. This tiered walkway designs space with an undulating arrangement of structural shapes.

Alternating motifs produce a rhythmical pattern. Stained glass window design by a Santiago High School student, California.

Half-Drop or Alternating Pattern

Pattern interest is developed by manipulating the placement of elements or motifs and, in particular, the spaces between elements. The grid pattern gives a uniform overall design quality. Other variations are possible by simply moving elements out of line by dropping or raising them so that they alternate regularly along a prescribed line. A half-drop design drops motifs half the height of themselves, giving an undulating look. Looking at these kinds of patterns, we can sense a feeling of movement that tends to increase as elements are spaced farther apart.

Take a simple shape, such as an inked slice of potato, and stamp a fairly open line of motifs. Then by printing the next line between the motifs half a space we create a half-drop pattern. Repeat this until you have covered an area with the half-drop pattern.

You can create an alternating pattern by following the same procedure, but you are not limited to half-space arrangements. Alternating patterns can be groupings of motifs along one line with a different number of motifs either above or below that line. Even the motifs may vary (in shape, size, color, and so on), but on a consistent basis: pattern requires a logical system of repetition with motifs.

Try a series of experiments with half-drop or alternating patterns using several media such as colored pencils and pen and ink, or black and white and colored construction paper. You can try many variations with cut paper motifs by shifting units around on the paper. When you find an arrangement you like, paste down the motifs.

Radial Pattern

As you know from the discussion of radial balance, to *radiate* means to branch out from a central point. Star shapes, asterisks, wheel spokes, and fireworks bursting in the air are radial patterns; each element or lineal unit extends from the center outward. Usually the units occur in precise intervals or spaces. Radial patterns have an explosive quality and seem to accelerate our eye speed as we follow the enlargement of shapes as they move outward. Radial patterns are generally dynamic, active, and structurally strong.

In experiments with pattern development, the radial pattern affords an opportunity to create dynamic

movement. Small, bursting patterns might be contrasted with large, slowly accelerating radial designs. Such large designs can be created various ways. For example, you could gradually change value or color along each radiating unit, or break down a radiating line into dots or dashes that increase in size as they move outward. Tie-dyes also make exciting radial patterns.

Cut strips of colored tissue might be used to form radial patterns. Cut them into straight or tapered lineal shapes and use them singly or overlapped. Secure them to paper with liquid starch or gel medium (acrylic paint additive). Explore the house and garage as well as nature to find forms that have radial patterns. Use them to print or press in designed patterns. Your pattern making will take on a more adventurous look because movement in design quickly catches the eye with its dynamic formations.

When looking at this fan-shaped leaf form, we experience a rapid acceleration of the line elements as they move outward in radiating directions from a central core.

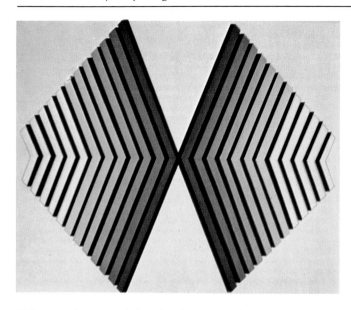

This experiment with bands of color, or value, gave this California State University, Fullerton, student an opportunity to explore numerous pattern arrangements.

Bands of colorful fabrics make dining accessories like tablecloths and napkins rich visual elements. Often such treatments are coordinated to unify effects. Photograph courtesy of Marimekko Designs.

Borders and Bands

A popular approach to adding pattern to many of the things we use in life is to enrich surfaces with borders or bands of decorative design. These added decorations seem to add a feeling of elegance and individuality. Throughout history sports teams have used bands and borders of color and design to identify themselves. Clothing, cars, trains, planes, pottery, and household items are just a few of the things that we often see decorated with either bands of color or borders of pattern. Borders and bands will emphasize the edge of a form or set apart a particular area, somewhat like underlining a word to make it more important. Once you put a border around a shape, you make it visually stronger.

The possibilities for border or band decoration are numerous. Patterns can develop by just grouping a series of bands that form lineal or shape patterns. These bands could be equally spaced or alternately grouped (for example, five bands, space, two bands, space, five bands). Different thicknesses, color and value changes, and patterns can increase the visual interest of a border.

It is fascinating to watch someone making pots on a potter's wheel, to observe the banding of depressions in clay formed from finger pressure. Banding pots or three-dimensional pieces with colored slips or glazes is an excellent way to achieve decorative patterns.

Painters often use mechanical devices, such as tapes or stencils, to produce hard-edge painting effects. Try using drafting tape of various widths (¼ inch, ⅜ inch, ½ inch) to break up a piece of watercolor paper into well-spaced divisions. After fitting the tapes securely, paint in areas of watercolor, varying intensities and values. When the paint is dry, carefully remove tapes to reveal clean white areas and hard-edged color areas. On quality watercolor paper this process can be repeated one or two more times to build rich, transparent watercolor overlays.

Border patterns are suitable to many design solutions. Emphasizing an edge of fabric or a clothing item with an attractive border of pattern visually strengthens the shape. The border may be used to emphasize one area, such as a neckline or the edge of a sleeve. It can surround and reinforce the edges of the total shape. What types of borders would you add to a king's or queen's robe? What kinds of shapes, lines, and colors would you use on a border for a side panel on a racing car?

Rhythmical Pattern

Rhythm is another of the organizing art principles that we can use to produce eye-catching patterns. Like the rhythmical beat of music (or the coordinated rhythms of dancers), pattern that moves along curved, circular, or undulating paths will produce a visual motion that moves our eyes along prescribed directions. We sense a flowing action in rhythmical pattern. Each motif seems to move easily to the next unit throughout the total flow of the design.

We see many rhythmical patterns in nature: the swirling patterns on sea shells and grained wood, wave action on the sea, blown patterns on the sand, and land erosion by wind and water. Contour land plowing and harvesting create large, rhythmical patterned land forms that look like oversized canvases or designs from the air. Weather satellites' pictures show rhythmical patterns of storms where clouds swirl in consistent directional paths.

To make rhythmical patterns, a designer may break up areas into lineal movements that curve in and out, in arcs, or in wavelike actions. Such movement guidelines can then be the paths that the motif pattern units are applied to. The rhythm or movement becomes the overriding organizational or unifying factor. Some rhythms may be slight and easy to read. Others can be extremely complex, interweaving, and changing in pace. Pattern motifs may be conditioned in size by the tightness or looseness of the rhythmical arcs. Much of the optical art today utilizes rhythmical patterns that produce strong visual sensations.

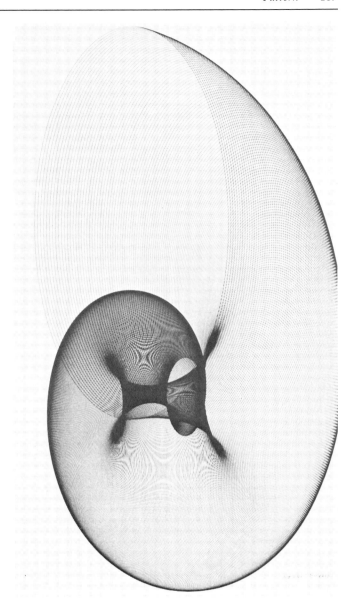

Computers can be turned into pattern producers. Note the lineal rhythms and emerging moiré patterns. Courtesy of Calcomp, Anaheim, California.

Giacomo Balla, a dynamic painter of the Futurist movement, capitalized on rhythmical pattern to present strong visual movements in this painting. *Swifts: Paths of Movement and Dynamic Sequences,* 1913, oil on canvas (38⅛″ x 47¼″). Collection, The Museum of Modern Art, New York.

Besides discovering the many rhythmical patterns in nature and manufactured objects, consider patterns placed into rhythmical frameworks. With paint or drawing media, explore patterns that move in vertical arcs, across horizontal paths, in concentric circles, or along wavelike grids. Adapt your motifs to fit the movement. Decrease some in size as a pattern movement contracts. Expand the motif as the movement opens up. Rhythm is an easy way to tie together units so that the patterns formed are both optically intriguing and well organized.

Pattern and Materials

As we watch a carpenter nailing siding to the front of a house, observe a bricklayer fitting blocks together for a wall, or see a basketweaver bending strips of reed, we are looking at the growth of patterns from materials.

The materials we use to make a pattern determine how we produce the pattern, whether by stacking, bending, folding, tying, or molding. Each material has its own unique potential for pattern, and the artist, craftsperson, or artisan knows the nature and possibilities of such materials. Steel is usually rigid, so it is cut and welded to fashion forms or structures. Sculptors enjoy its strength and attack it with welding torches, power grinders, sanders, and buffers. Swirling patterns are made by the grinding process on metal. Angular patterns are produced from welding pieces together.

The potter presses clay together to form patterns, or covers a surface with glaze patterns. Weavers knit patterns from fibers and fabrics that compress together or stretch apart depending on the desired look. You can see that many patterns can be built into the materials themselves, or can be built in the processes of using materials.

Once you have experimented with materials to get the "feel" of what they can do, you can start to create the design and patterns that seem to belong to those materials. In working with wood, you may see the possibilities of emphasizing the pattern of the grain by sanding and staining. The British sculptor Henry Moore often used wood grain in his work to achieve a moving pattern throughout a sculptural piece. In hammered metal, each indentation helps to form a

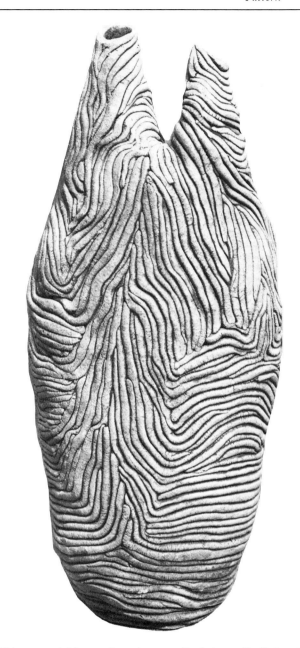

This eye-catching pattern is a result of clay coils fit together to build a ceramic pot. Villa Park High School, California.

Woven materials, whether fabric or reed, use interlacing patterns to build structural unity and aesthetic qualities.

Ink line describes forms and establishes a flowing pattern. Study by Santiago High School student, California.

pattern. Carving or bending can make an in-and-out pattern.

Study materials to see if you can discover the possibilities for attractive patterns. Certain materials give obvious pattern results, whereas other materials can be modified to produce pattern. You can use certain tools either to create patterns or to emphasize patterns that are already there.

The fascination of working with materials that offer a wealth of pattern possibilities will add to your previous experiments in pattern development.

The materials of art are highly diverse today, ranging from paper to plastics. As artists and students of art, we need to explore these materials to open the creative channels for design and pattern development.

Pattern in Nature

The greatest inspiration for pattern development and discovery is nature. The more you observe the endless kinds of pattern in nature, the easier it will be to transfer those impressions into your own creative work. Some of your observation should take in the broad sweep of the landscape, or of larger forms like trees and mountains. Also look for the sectional details that provide intriguing visual information. You can readily see the patterns in major shapes like groups of trees or cloud-filled skies, but you can also find the smaller, more intimate patterns of nature's forms, such as the veins of leaves, the textured patterns of small pebbles, or the ridges in water-washed sand.

Try carefully searching one small section of your landscape for pattern formations. You will find that even grassy areas can have patterns, such as those that are formed when the wind blows in one major direction. The surfaces on rocks, exposed earth, tree bark, or ruffled water all deliver patterned messages, each unique and related to its own specific quality. Look at the insides of flowers or seed pods to uncover hidden patterns.

You might take along a sketchbook to record patterns, sections of patterns, or motifs. Or you could use

The peacock's plumage is a spectacular radial pattern. Note the eyelike motifs and underlying lineal structure.

a camera to give you a permanent reference of the most appealing patterns. Along with looking and sketching, discern the types of pattern you see and the senations you get from certain patterns. What types of rhythms and repeated units can you see? Does the pattern reflect the growth of a form? Is the pattern a protective or hiding device? How does it enhance the form? Can you find similar patterns in other areas of nature?

Your notebook or memory file can include such factors as type, sizes, and sequences of pattern: appropriateness to the form; and the details or motifs that make up a pattern. Experiment with different art media to help extend your impressions into imaginative directions.

Pattern and Design

The desire to decorate is innate. We enjoy changing our visual world by adding things we buy or make. Pattern is an important visual item in the things we acquire and enjoy.

To design means to organize, simplify, and arrange the elements of art such as line, shape and form, color, value, texture, and space. To make a pattern is to juggle these elements so that they work effectively with our chosen materials.

Painters, sculptors, graphic designers, interior designers, landscape architects, architects, fashion designers, photographers, and film-makers all use pattern. In fact, the list could be extended into most of industry and product manufacture. As buyers we should be discriminating in our choices so that patterns work well together, seem appropriate for the effect we wish to achieve, and provide visual variety.

We prefer some patterns to be subtle and to totally integrate with the object; we want others to be bold and invigorating. In designing your own room, the selection of rich pattern can provide a liveliness that cannot be achieved by mere color alone. Try a change of mood in your personal space by adding some unique patterns, either on purchased items or your own creations.

This ability to design or visually control your own environment reinforces your understanding of pattern and reflects your personal judgment. When you become homeowners or apartment dwellers, the selection and use of designed pattern will have a pronounced effect on the quality of your visual life.

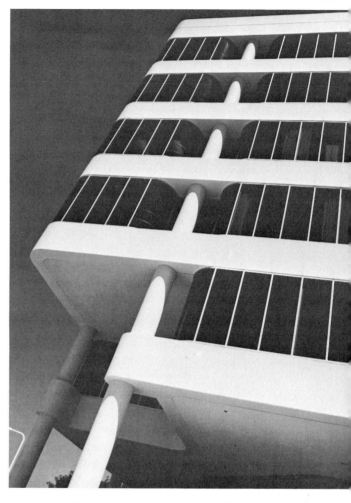

A clean, unified design is often the result of the arrangements of shapes and lines, which form well-defined patterns. Architectural photograph by Julius Schulman.

Pattern exploration may be printed units, rhythmical line areas, or painted motifs. Pattern's diversity offers a wide variety of creative solutions.

Other Design Projects

Putting pattern into action is the most enjoyable aspect of understanding this principle of design. Your experiences in seeing and being aware of pattern and how it functions will probably whet your appetite to try your hand at creating and using pattern. You may want to start with relatively simple exercises in producing pattern, such as lines of repeated shapes or grouping swatches of color. As your skill and preference decide, you can move to complex pattern constructions with paint, print media, or three-dimensional materials. You might try some trial sketches to test possibilities. From these initial drawings, your ideas can develop and imaginative expression can take over.

As you increase your pattern skills, look also at the work of artists who made pattern an integral part of their work. This research, along with your own sketchbook activities, will stimulate a great number of pattern possibilities. The following list of suggested activities should help you understand the role of pattern as a dynamic design principle and develop skill in using it.

List and briefly describe at least ten different patterns you have viewed during one day.

Make a series of rubbings (soft pencil rubbed over a paper placed over an object) that pick up unique patterns. Try wood grains, concrete patterns, metal objects, and fiber surfaces.

Cut and arrange a series of different patterns that demonstrate simple repeats, grids, half-drop patterns, and radial and spiral designs.

Cut patterns into linoleum, plaster blocks, or clay (which should be fired before using), and print several repeated units on paper. Make variations with unique inking (several colors or values), overlapping, and different paper surfaces.

Construct a sculptural form from a repeated modular unit (such as small cylindrical pill bottles or small boxes). Try staggering or alternating units to give an interesting relief look.

Weave a pattern of shapes or forms into a unified design. For these designs you may use colored paper, threads and fibers, tubing or metal parts, or a mixture of mechanical and organic forms.

Eraser prints and ink pads or paint can produce quick pattern results. By using several eraser sizes (art gums are easily cut into many printing shapes) and round pencil erasers, you can make a number of unusual patterns. Printed fingers and thumbs add another possibility for pattern development.

Draw or paint linear patterns with several implements that give different widths or textures (shaped pencil points, flexible pens, felt pens and markers, and so on). Compact some patterns; open up other areas. Try criss-crossing and grouping lines.

Draw or paint animals or human forms and break the major shapes into areas for exaggerated patterns.

Movement and Rhythm

Movement is used by a designer to lead our eyes in many ways—changing the mood by "gliding" us across a section of the artwork, then stopping us abruptly with a strategically placed line or color. Perhaps weaving forms or shapes in a particular way will give a sense of falling and then of regaining visual equilibrium. Rhythm is produced by repeating one or several visual elements in a work of art.

Rhythm and movement in art may be simple or complex, much as the rhythm and movement of music range from a tune we whistle after a "single listen" to the complex forms of a symphonic piece. In writing, rhythm and movement may be found in a simple limerick or a more complex poem or short story.

Action and Pictures of Action

If a squirrel just picked up some peanuts outside the door, ate several and carried the rest away to bury in his favorite hiding place, that is *action*. If you took a photograph of the squirrel running away, that would be a *picture of action*. The still black-and-white photograph can remind you of action, but no *real* action exists in the picture.

Physical action means that a change of position or location takes place. The squirrel moves and changes his location. A single photograph cannot change location of itself, and even several sequential photographs cannot actually move. All a drawing, photograph, or painting of the squirrel can do is provide a record of action, but not action itself.

There are various forms of pictures of action; photographs are the most common. Vapor trails etched across a deep blue sky can indicate action (change of position). Severely folded layers of rock in a highway cut is the visual record of monumental action, and the active force of moving water can be read in an eroded hillside. These are not actions, however, but are visual records of actions that have taken place.

Art That Is Action

Alexander Calder was not satisfied with attempts to imply action in an unmovable piece of work. After some experimentation, he devised a type of sculpture that actually moves: a mobile.

Alexander Calder, *Lobster Trap and Fish Tail*, 1939. Collection, The Museum of Modern Art, New York.

The action is halted by the camera, but the blurred images suggest action and force.

Marcel Duchamp expressed action by using a multiple image, similar to a stop-action photograph series. *Nude Descending a Staircase,* 1912 (58″ x 35″). Philadelphia Museum of Art, Louise and Walter Arensberg Collection.

There are other types of art that are not merely representations of action, but really change positions. Some are motorized, while others use gravity to produce action. Some move rapidly and others almost imperceptibly. Some are large, others small. Some use moving lights while others use moving steel parts. Some are programmed and others have to be started manually. This type of art that uses actively moving parts is called *kinetic* art.

Baroque sculptors, wanting to get the most movement possible in their work, often combined them with moving water and produced elaborate fountains. The surface of the carved marble appeared to have an action of its own. If the water can be considered part of the work, the sculptures actually did move.

Implied Action

One of the marvelous qualities of your eye is that it can shift itself to follow action. A car speeding across your plane of vision might be picked up on the left and followed to the right. If your eye were fixed (like a still camera lens) and could not move, your vision would record only a blur, which you would probably not even recognize as a car.

Blurred photographs imply action; strobe lights can stop action in several parts of a continuous movement and record a multiple image on a single piece of film, thus implying action. In a work of art or photograph, limp materials (leaves, flags, banners, smoke) imply action when they flap or show the effects of a forceful wind. An artist trying to communicate action may use several of these devices to get the message across.

Graphic Movement

Action Versus Movement

The previous pages have given an overview of various types of action, but this section will deal with movement and rhythm. It is difficult to explain what graphic movement is unless you understand action. Graphic movement is *not* action. Action is an actual physical change in position. In art, movement is experienced by comparing the positions of stationary objects in relation to each other within the borders of a picture.

By photographing up this airplane hangar ladder, a strong sense of movement is created by the angled lines. Photograph by Walt Selleck.

Our eye is quickly drawn to the figure in the lower right of this watercolor by Dorothy Rennie. However, we then begin to take a visual path down the figure's right arm, then up the left part of the picture and over to the sculptured face. Then we notice the many smaller paths and details.

A picket fence cannot move, but it definitely has movement as it leads your eye from one picket to the next. As you notice the change of position of objects in a photograph or painting and their relationship to each other, you are becoming aware of graphic movement. Graphic movement can be generated by tensions, imbalance, tilting, running lines, arrow shapes, and other devices.

Movement on the Picture Plane

Most of the time, a painting or photograph will contain shapes, lines, textures, and/or colors. An artist will use these design elements to lead your eye over a prescribed course in a designated movement.

The blank sheet of paper or canvas on which you begin to work is already generating graphic movement. The corners of the sheet are shaped like arrow tips and your eye will move over the void to one of the four corners. Without special instructions, your eye will generally move across a clean sheet from left to right (the way you are taught to read) and head for the upper right corner (the first place to exit). A single small dot, placed near one of the corners, will move your eye in that direction. Try it!

Vertical lines in Gothic architecture lead the eye upward. Notice how many times the vertical lines are repeated in this tower.

Since graphic movement is already present on a blank sheet, it is up to the artist to produce controlled movement that will lead to a desired point in the work. Such control of movement is essential to all pictures. Without it, there is chaos and disorganization, and the picture will fall apart structurally.

As seen and discussed in Chapter 1, vertical, horizontal, and diagonal aspects of a design have certain characteristics, purposes, and moods.

Vertical Movement

Gothic architects, trying to lead the eyes of worshippers toward God, built the naves of their cathedrals as high as possible to develop a vertical movement or feeling—from the individual to God. They enhanced such movement by duplicating vertical lines as often as possible, using ribs in columns, decorative lines on spires, and vertically shaped windows with pointed arches. All served to strengthen the upward sense of movement.

While most pictures with vertical movement are also vertical in shape, it is not essential that they be so. Horizontal compositions can also contain strong vertical movement.

Straight-line vertical compositions can be very strong in their sense of movement and might easily carry the viewer out of the picture. Artists can overcome this by blocking such movement with a few horizontal lines or shapes that help contain the movement within the frame.

Horizontal Movement

If you drop your pencil on the table, it will assume a horizontal position. When you are tired, you lie down flat to rest. When a tree topples over, it comes to rest on the ground. The standing tree was in balance, the falling tree was out of balance, and the horizontal tree is at rest. Gravity pulls it flat to the surface of the earth.

If an artist wants to show quiet, peace, and rest, she or he will probably use a horizontal composition with horizontal movement dominating the work. Horizontal graphic movement is strengthened because it is parallel to the top and bottom borders of the picture. This reinforcement of horizontality causes such compositions to be quiet, strong, and at rest. Often they will cause the viewer to feel secure.

Most horizontal compositions move from left to right, the way we read a sentence. The horizon line and eye levels, both basic factors in our personal relationship to the earth, are capable of producing horizontal movement.

Since movement along a horizontal course is quite rapid, it is often desirable to have one or two verticals that will anchor the composition and keep the movement from running off the edge of the page. This can sometimes be done subtly with a delicate color or textural change that merely suggests vertical movement.

Diagonal Movement

If vertical movement produces a feeling of balance and horizontal movement produces an attitude of rest, then *diagonal* movement should provide a sense of unrest or action. Generally, it does. Of course, some diagonal compositions do not show people or things in action, but the diagonal arrangement of the parts of the picture will generate a feeling of uneasiness, imbalance and implied action. Counter-diagonals will help stabilize the composition and bring it back into a feeling of balance.

An artist who wants to show action will use diagonal movement to reinforce the action. Medieval artists were accustomed to portraying static figures, using vertical movement. Renaissance painters, wanting to show a more active and natural world, used many diagonals to help express such action.

The trees provide vertical movement, but the main movement is horizontal because of the position of the figure— she rests and is centrally located in the painting, though her head is off-center, and is the center of interest. Will Barnet, *Summer Idyll,* oil on canvas (41″ x 53″). Courtesy of Hirschil and Adler Galleries, New York.

If you want to show action in your work, in sculpture, painting or drawing, diagonal movement will help you achieve that feeling. A stable, vertical shape (like a building) can appear more active by rotating it slightly (tilting it one way or the other) and making it somewhat diagonal. A forest of straight trees can be more exciting if the trunks are tipped a bit to make them more dynamic. Backgrounds can also be rotated to make the entire composition more active.

What Direction Does It Take?

Movement implies action in some direction, and several factors determine which way our eye moves in a picture.

An object's shape will give a clue about its direction of movement. If it is longer in one dimension than another, the movement will be along the longer dimension. But the major *direction* is often determined by surrounding shapes, lines, and values.

Our eye seems to move along progressions: small shapes to large, light values to dark, smooth to rough, fat to thin, generalizations to detail.

Some objects are arrow-shaped and point us in the right direction (some artists even use arrows in their paintings). Some shapes have a definite front and back (autos, planes, fish, animals), and the direction of movement will usually be similar to the direction the object is pointed. Some artists move our eyes around by having us follow pointing fingers or the gaze of one person looking toward another.

Objects which are placed close to edges of pictures seem to move toward these borders (and usually out of the picture), so care must be taken to direct the movement inward, toward a center of interest, if that is the artist's desire.

When first looking at a picture, we seem to notice the large shapes first. Our eyes move along each axis and around the shape as the artist directs us. Soon we begin to examine the details and notice that each object has its own set of movements, determined by lines, shadows, colors, or textures. So we first see the largest movements and then begin to discover the smaller, more subtle movements in various areas of the work. This is part of the excitement of discovery in art.

Line and Shape Movement

As you drive down the highway, your eye follows the yellow lines on the pavement. Your eye follows the lines of white vapor trails in a blue sky or dark telephone lines spanning space. Some cities have scenic routes marked by a blue line that leads from one visual or historic attraction to another.

It is difficult to keep from following a line. As we have seen, artists use lines in their work to direct eye movement to a desired location. Whether the line might be subtle or bold, broken or solid, as a design element it has a strong influence on graphic movement.

A *shape* can have movement of its own if it is longer than it is wide. If the shape is pointed at one end, the movement can even be directional. Several shapes in one composition immediately set up a relationship that produces movement between them, regardless of their individual shapes. When you begin to notice these relationships and tensions between shapes, you will be aware of graphic movement.

An elongated shape tends to produce movement along its axis (a line drawn through the center of the shape lengthwise), and we read the movement almost like we read a line.

Because shapes have edges, our eyes often find it easier to follow the movement of the lines that graphically form these edges. We also tend to read long, thin shapes like heavy lines, and follow their movements quite easily.

Shapes can be distorted or bent to become more active. An artist who wants to express the movement and congestion of an urban area might bend buildings in a painting to make them match the hustle and bustle of the people.

The dots of lights lead our eye over the scene, and we pause to look longer where they cluster or where other details are more easily seen.

The interweaving of wheels, lines, spokes, and shadows creates a fascinating visual movement.

This plastic shoe bag displays the store's monogram, which is designed to produce a feeling of continuous movement.

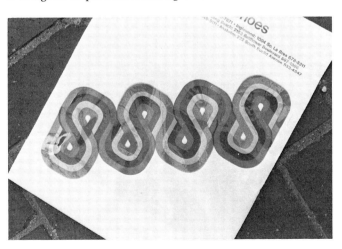

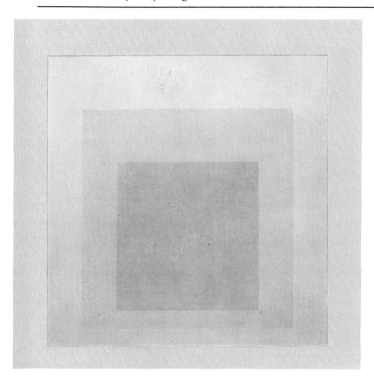

Squares of different values that are similar in color are placed on top of each other with the largest square being the highest on the page. The edges are hard and soft, and the shapes seem to blend, intersect, and visually move with a "push-and-pull" effect. Gaze at the picture for a few moments and see if these sensations exist for you. Josef Albers, *Beyond Focus*, 1969, oil on masonite. Los Angeles County Museum of Art, promised gift of Mr. and Mrs. Taft Schreiber.

Value Movement

Artists can use value to generate movement in three ways: by passage through similar values that touch each other, by transition from dark to light or light to dark, and by skipping from one place to another place of similar value. Artists who can effectively control values in their work lead us through various routes to the points of emphasis or centers of interest.

Our eye moves over values that are comparatively the same, so we find ourselves seeking a route through a painting that ties together similar values. In nature and in a flat photograph or painting, we can often find places on one object that have values similar to a background. This similarity creates a visual relationship between the background and the object. We call this common area a *passage*. Whether the values are light, medium, or dark, your eye can transfer from one object to another or from the positive object to the background by following similar values.

Another movement generated by value involves a *transition* up or down the value scale. Our eyes tend to move over the surface of a round form from light to dark or dark to light. We move easily from light gray to medium gray to medium-dark gray to dark gray to black. It is similar to moving up or down a ladder.

We can also sense movement as we *skip* from one value to a similar value in another part of the picture. These isolated values become shapes, and our eyes move in a line directly from one to another.

Similar colors can lead us through a painting in a particular movement. Contrasting colors create a different kind of movement—some seeming to come forward, some receding. Find some examples in this painting, *Space Shot,* by James Fuller.

Color Movement

We have already discussed how warm colors advance (move forward) and cool colors recede (move back) in a painting. Bright colors seem closer to us than pale or muted colors, which seem to move away.

Like values, color can cause a variety of movements in a composition. If orange appears in the foreground bricks and then shows up again in several flower patches and in the tile roof of a house, you can feel the movement from one patch of orange to another.

A less obvious movement may develop if the artist uses related or analogous colors instead of exactly the same hues—perhaps red-orange in the bricks, yellow-orange in the flowers, and red in the tiles of the roof. With red present in all the hues, our eyes would move from one red-related hue to the others throughout the work.

A series of warm colors in cool surroundings will cause movement from warm to warm, even if the hues are not the same. A group of light-valued splashes of color will produce movement on a dark-valued background, regardless of the hues.

Like value movement, colors will move along a series of changes in hue if there is a relationship along each step. To generate movement from a green grassy area to a bright red building, an artist can develop a visual bridge by gradually changing the green grass in places to green-brown to brown to red-brown to red. Such a passage will produce movement in the direction of the center of interest, the house.

Color and value can work together to provide passage from one area to another. Light-valued green can move directly to a light-valued orange that touches it if they are surrounded by medium or dark values of any color. Movement is probably produced more by value than by color. If values lack contrast, however, color will produce movement by itself.

The highlights on the arms and the folds of the clothing help to create movement along the curving forms by providing a visual path. David Alfaro Siqueiros, *Portrait of a Woman*, 1934, oil on masonite (59½" x 30¾"). Los Angeles County Museum of Art, gift of Morton D. May.

Spanish architect Antonio Gaudi designed this Barcelona apartment with an undulating surface. Your eye cannot move in a straight line, but moves in and out along the sculptured surfaces. Baroque architecture used similar principles, but was more ordered, while Gaudi's becomes almost free-form. Courtesy of the Ministerio de Informacion y Turismo.

By placing the figures high in the picture, the photographer creates a strong rush of movement from the empty lower area toward the top.

Other Ways to Produce Movement

Artists can use still other devices to generate movement. For example, the artist can move parts of a scene around to create relationships that will clarify the pattern of movement.

Cézanne rearranged nature in his work to produce a more pleasing design—a more clearly established path on which to move. The cubists positioned the various parts of their works to enhance movement, and most abstractionists simply place their colors, shapes, or lines in locations that seem exactly right to them, and produce relationships that are personally satisfying.

Several other ways to show movement might include:

- overlapping objects to produce movement from one to the other.
- aligning edges (contours) to produce the feeling of continuous movement along its edges.
- developing a strong sense of *form*, so the eye seems to go around and *behind* the objects in a three-dimensional movement.
- creating a path between objects in which movement seems to flow.
- by rotating or tilting the picture plane to establish a sense of urgency and action.
- by emphasizing or exaggerating certain lines or colors in order to draw attention to the pattern of movement.
- placing the horizon line high in the picture to emphasize movement *up* to the center of interest.

Eye Movement in Sculpture

In viewing sculpture, our eyes generally move over contours that the artist has carved or molded to produce continuous movement to the center of interest. In some ways, the sculptor's job is more difficult than the painter's because the sculptor works in three dimensions and the movement in sculpture must read from all points of view. The skilled sculptor directs our eye over, through, and around his work in a way that complements the form and basic idea of the piece. Put simply, if the artist wants a sense of deliberate, slow movement, he or she *isn't* going to use shapes, lines, and textures that will "hurry us" so much that we miss the point of interest.

Eye Movement in Architecture

Ancient Greeks tried to produce public buildings of great beauty (such as the Parthenon). Their concept of beauty was concerned with proportion and movement—the ease and comfort with which the eye could survey the structure.

Contemporary architects are also concerned with visual movement that successfully coordinates the various parts of their designs. They use lines, shapes, textures, shadows, contours, and colors to lead our eyes over the surface or around the edges. Movement is directed to encompass the building and its immediate environment (including fountains, trees, rocks, and so on) and lead *into* the structure.

Some buildings reflect their surroundings, and the reflection is included in the visual movement. Others might have reflecting pools that mirror the building. This actually produces noticeable movement as the viewer passes by.

When several structures are clustered together, it is important to notice the visual movement from one to the other, strengthening the feeling of unity. Planning is therefore extremely important in producing a sense of togetherness in a cluster of buildings—exactly the same sense that persists in a well-designed sculpture. Can you find groups of structures in your town or city that seem to "go well together"? Maybe, if you sketch them, you can determine why they seem comfortable in a group.

Rhythm

The band starts to play and your foot begins to tap or you drum your fingers on the table. Your piano teacher wants you to follow the time strictly. You are happy when spring rolls around again, or when the last bell rings, or when the sun goes down. The coach or captain shouts out numbers and the push-ups must be done on the count. The hammer pounds. The oars are pulled. The tides come and go. As patterns of action develop, so does rhythm.

Rhythm is the organized repetition of visual movement, an organization that is built around repetitions of color, shape, value movements, or lines. Rhythm is fundamental to our lives. We are surrounded by rhythms. We learn to walk, run, dance, talk, and eat in patterns of repetition.

Authors of books and directors of motion pictures sustain interest by having alternating periods of excitement and quiet, suspense and relief. These are rhythmic patterns. You probably couldn't tolerate a complete book if it were entirely high-pitched excitement.

We tend to appreciate regular rhythmic occurrences because they are predictable and contribute to order and stability. If rhythms are *too* much the same, we might judge them to be monotonous. If all the downtown high-rise buildings were exactly the same height and shape, they would present a dull skyline. Many of our neighborhoods are uninteresting because of look-alike houses or apartments. As you learned in the discussion about artistic unity, *variety* of size, color, or shape helps overcome such boredom.

When things become too predictable or repetitious, we seem to dismiss them as unexciting or dull. So, an artist might *want* to express boredom by repeating exactly the same size and shape and color, as Andy Warhol did in his exhibit of Campbell Soup can paintings.

If stimulation is to be retained, variety is vital to visual rhythm. Alternations can be made within the rhythmic pattern by changing sizes, colors, exact shapes, positions, values, and/or direction of the repeated items, or the intervals between them.

Curved strips of paper are controlled and glued to the backing in this student project. Shadows and highlights help distinguish the flowing rhythm.

Types of Rhythm

Smooth and Flowing Rhythm

The samba, rumba, frug, bump, waltz, or any other dance step is danced to its own rhythm because the beat is different in each type of music. Composers try to match the rhythm with the mood or verbal characteristic of the selection. Poets use rhythm in arranging the words and syllables of their work. Artists, using visual movement and rhythms, work in a similar way.

Rhythms can be smooth, rough, jagged, isolated, sporadic, interacting, and so on. Each rhythm is capable of conveying a feeling or mood. If quiet and serenity are to be shown, the artist will not use hard and jagged rhythms and movement, but might try to express the mood with soft, flowing lines that weave back and forth across the work.

Smooth, flowing movements seem to blend the whole composition together in a peaceful but powerful way. They are usually large movements that sweep across the entire work, tying each of the parts in a free and flowing fashion. Artists might use such rhythms in landscapes or figure work. But they might just as easily use them in completely abstract compositions that communicate smoothness and unity.

Staccato and Angular Rhythm

While repeating flowing lines and/or shapes produces a feeling of smooth interaction with one part flowing into the next, sharp and jagged rhythms cause completely opposite feelings.

Acute angles, not present in most free-flowing movement, add to the sharpness and crispness of angular rhythms. Excitement, contact, suspense, confusion, power, or action can be conveyed through jerky, irregular, radical, or energetic rhythms.

Both commercial and fine artists make use of such combinations to produce a given feeling in their work. Constant practice and experimentation will help you determine which rhythms work best in certain situations. Can you fill several pages with line drawings that simply express several different rhythms?

Eye movement is from right to left along the top of the fence, and a rhythm is set up because of alternating heavy posts and smaller slats and also because of the dipping curves of the top edge.

The rhythms of crowded boats at a marina are emphasized in this abstract watercolor by Perry Owen.

Repetition of graceful arcs helps tie together the parts of San Xavier del Bac church. Notice how the architect sustained interest by varying the size of the arcs and inverting some of them (variety within unity). Can you find other repeated shapes, forms, or lines that help create a unified effect?

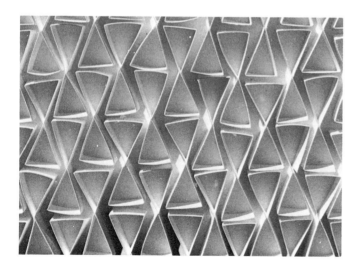

Benches are arranged in a regular rhythmic order to produce an overall pattern. The alternating dark and light colors add another rhythm.

Repeated triangular paper forms produce a regular rhythm in this student paste-up project. The assignment called for repeating a single unit to cover a surface with pattern.

Regular Rhythm Equals Pattern

When the size, shape, and color of the *repeated* units remain the same and the *intervals* between the units are constant, the rhythm is regular and predictable, forming a repeated pattern. Such organizations may be restricted to borders or edges or they may be over-all patterns, covering the entire surface of a building or a sheet of wrapping paper.

Architects and designers may use pattern to develop a sense of unity and to produce an almost textural surface. If either the size, shape, or color of the units is changed, the pattern is broken, but it can also be broken by varying the intervals or spaces between the units. The pattern then becomes *random* and is no longer predictable. This concept is discussed in greater detail on page 181.

Irregular Rhythm: The Unexpected

As already mentioned, variety is an important factor in visual rhythm. Excitement in our lives is often the result of some unexpected happening or series of events. In visual rhythm also, the unexpected can add suspense and tension to the work and increase its interest. Variation in size, color and/or shape of units can result in unpredictable patterns, as can the irregular spacing of the intervals between units. If all the windows in a building are dark, the pattern is dull; but if several are light, the interest increases. It would increase more if the windows were placed at random in the wall.

Designers generally like the exciting possibilities they can generate when the rhythm in their work varies from place to place. They can speed up the graphic movement, slow it down, make it skip around, and finally make it stop at the center of interest.

Variety is often desirable, but it must be controlled through the use of repetitive units or it will turn into chaos.

Look at the top of the fire escape stairway. The spaces between each step are fairly equal as you visually work your way down. But then the large, black shape of the platform interrupts. The pattern picks up again as you continue down, but because of the poles in the background, the spaces between the steps are broken into smaller rectangles—a good example of irregular rhythm. Try a design based on this idea.

Follow the "rhythm and movement paths" created by the artist's placement of legs, arms and faces. Mary Cassatt, *Mother About to Wash Her Sleepy Child*, 1880, oil on canvas (39½" x 25¾"). Los Angeles County Museum of Art, Bequest of Mrs. Fred Hathaway Bixby.

Notice how visual elements are balanced. Does the peaked roof direct your eye like an arrow? Can you find the two ways that the artist gets your eye back down to the television set? Norman Rockwell, *The New Television Set*, 1949, oil on canvas (53½" x 42½"). Los Angeles County Museum of Art, gift of Mrs. Ned Crowell.

Other Design Projects

Study a reproduction of a famous painting. Then ask yourself these questions: "How does the artist lead my eye through and around the painting? Is it accomplished mainly with line, color, shapes, or values?"

Construct a simple mobile using a variety of sizes, shapes, and lengths of wire or thread. Try to vary the spaces between the shapes as well. How will the kinds of shapes you use affect the sense of movement and rhythm? Begin working with the bottom elements first.

Cut six or seven simple long, thin rectangles from one sheet of construction paper. Place them horizontally on another colored sheet. Notice the restful mood created by the horizontal composition. Now add a few vertical long, thin rectangles of a third color *over* the horizontal rectangles. Your eye movement should change dramatically and the design's mood should alter. When the vertical rectangles overlap the horizontal ones, they form shapes out of the background color. Do these shapes lead your eye in any way? What rhythm or movement has developed in your design?

Listen to various kinds of music with a definite beat—rock, Hawaiian, South American, country-west-ern, and so on. Can you, with a few well-chosen colors and brush strokes, suggest those various rhythms and movements in a design?

Without using any recognizable objects, let a simple shape *represent* a figure and allow a line to take the "figure" on a journey that takes different directions and paths. As the line makes a dramatic change, cut out or draw the figure shape differently to symbolize the "change" he or she might take in mood, weariness, frustration, and so on.

Have a model take a simple pose—standing with a guitar, for example. Draw the model from one angle, emphasizing line. Now view the model from another direction, using a *different* color or drawing medium. Draw the new pose right *over* the first one. Then draw one more pose from a third angle, using a third kind of line right over the first two. Does your drawing suggest movement? Do the overlapping poses develop a rhythm? Can you add anything to your drawing to emphasize rhythm or movement? Will color help? Will pattern or texture or value help?

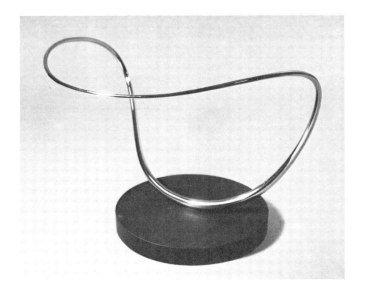

This design made with a forged rod of stainless steel is so delicately and elegantly formed and balanced that its simplicity is deceiving. Let your eye follow the rhythm and movement created by the loop. If you could move around this sculpture, the reflections on the shiny surface would move. José de Rivera, *Construction 8*, 1954 (9⅜" high). Collection, The Museum of Modern Art, New York, gift of Mrs. Heinz Schultz.

A major user of design is industry. This carefully thought-out machine, produced by Beckman Instruments, focuses on function and clarity.

Airports are critically designed structures that attain a design elegance by the treatment of shapes, line flow, and pattern.

Your eye loops over and around this granite sculpture by Max Bill.

Conclusion What Do We Do Now?

This design text is meant to bring you into contact with the elements and principles of design, to sharpen both your ideas and skills in design processes, and to expose you to the work of fellow students, professionals, and the world of design around us. It is intended as a starting process, not as an end in itself, because design and art are—and always have been—changing and adapting to a new world. We hope some of you will become some of those new designers that will help change life and the quality of visual expressiveness that design demands. As designers you will engage in many of the factors that profoundly affect people, whether it is new architectural horizons or the improvement of the products we use.

Equally importantly, you will become more visually sensitive and discriminating in selecting and using design. Everyone makes design decisions, and we hope that this book and the study of design will make those decisions easier, clearer, and more spontaneous.

All of us should have a say in the design of our environment and speak out for the most effective use of design in our communities and our nation as a whole. As individuals we can influence those around us, primarily by the example of using quality design in our lives, and also by our ability to intelligently discuss the benefits of design.

We have seen the effect of designers and the supporters of design in changing the image of a country. Sweden is noted for its design in furniture, glass and crafts. Switzerland is a strong proponent of excellent graphic design. Japan produces elegantly designed electronic equipment. In our own country architectural elegance is a prominent feature. In a sense, design application has become a national pride and financially rewarding.

Since everything people produce reflects a design sensibility, it is important that all the positive aspects of quality design are used. When this takes place, design excellence is achieved and recognized.

When architects design symphony halls, acoustics are emphasized first. Once the sound problems are worked out, aesthetics or beauty are emphasized. Can you explain this set of priorities? Sydney Opera House, courtesy of the Australian Tourist Commission.

Bibliography

Ballinger, Louise B., and Thomas F. Vroman. *Design: Sources and Resources.* Reinhold Publishing Company, New York, 1965.

Brommer, Gerald F., et al. *The Design Concepts Series.* Davis Publications, Inc., Worcester, Mass., 1974–1975.
ELEMENTS OF DESIGN:
   Brommer, Gerald F. *Space.*
   Gatto, Joseph A. *Color and Value.*
   Horn, George F. *Texture.*
   Porter Albert W. *Shape and Form.*
   Selleck, Jack. *Line.*
PRINCIPLES OF DESIGN:
   Brommer, Gerald F. *Movement and Rhythm.*
   Gatto, Joseph A. *Emphasis.*
   Horn, George F. *Balance and Unity.*
   Porter, Albert W. *Pattern.*
   Selleck, Jack. *Contrast.*

Collier, Graham. *Form, Space and Vision.* Prentice-Hall, Englewood Cliffs, N.J., 1963.

Collingwood, R.G., *The Principles of Art.* Oxford University Press, New York, 1972.

de Sausmarez, Maurice. *Basic Design: The Dynamics of Visual Form.* Reinhold Publishing Corporation, New York, 1964.

Dondif, Donif A. *A Primer of Visual Literacy.* MIT Press, Cambridge, Mass., 1973.

Garrett, Lillian. *Visual Design: A Problem Solving Approach.* Van Nostrand Reinhold, New York, 1967.

Graham, Donald W. *Composing Pictures.* Van Nostrand Reinhold, New York, 1970.

Guyler, Vivian Varney. *Design in Nature.* Davis Publications, Inc., Worcester, Mass., 1970.

Hale, Nathan Cabot. *Abstraction in Art and Nature.* Watson-Guptill Publications, New York, 1972.

Kranz, Stewart and Robert Fisher. *The Design Continuum.* Van Nostrand Reinhold, New York, 1966.

Malcolm, Dorothea C. *Design: Elements and Principles.* Davis Publications, Inc., Worcester, Mass. 1972.

Palmer, Fredrich. *Visual Awareness.* Batsford, Ltd., London, 1972.

Parola, Rene. *Optical Art.* Reinhold, New York, 1969.

Sneum, Gunnar. *Teaching Design and Form.* Reinhold, New York, 1965.

Stribling, Mary. *Art from Found Materials.* Crown Publishers, New York, 1971.

Tritten, Gottfried. *Teaching Color and Form in Secondary School.* Van Nostrand Reinhold, New York, 1971.

Glossary of Design Terms

abstract art a style of art that shows objects, people, and/or places in simplified arrangements of shape, line, texture, and color, often geometrical. Sometimes abstract refers to *non-objective art.*

Abstract Expressionism a twentieth-century painting style that tries to express feelings and emotions through slashing, active brush strokes. Often called *action painting.*

aerial perspective a way of drawing that shows depth in space by such methods as overlapping objects, using lighter values for more distant objects, using less detail in distant objects, and using warm colors for nearer items.

aesthetic pertaining to a sense of what is beautiful and visually pleasing.

analogous colors colors that are next to each other on the color wheel. They are related because they contain a common hue. Yellow-green, yellow, and yellow-orange are analogous colors.

anatomy the structure of the human body (or of animals or plants). Anatomical drawing often shows such details as muscle and bones.

architect a person who develops plans for buildings, groups of buildings, communities, bridges, and so on.

architecture the design of buildings, such as homes, offices, schools, and industrial structures.

asymmetrical balance a type of visual balance in which one side of the composition appears different from the other side but is balanced with it. The two sides are visually equal without being identical.

Avant Garde art the style of contemporary art in any period of time. It is the newest form of visual expression, and farthest from the traditional ways of working.

back lighting a lighting arrangment in which the source of light is behind the subject, shining toward the viewer. It often produces a silhouette effect.

balance a principle of design that refers to the equalization of elements in a work of art. There are three kinds of balance: symmetrical (formal), asymmetrical (informal), and radial.

Bauhaus a German art school, begun in 1918, that stressed science and technology as major resources for art and architecture. Many contemporary concepts of design were originated at the Bauhaus.

blocking-in quickly sketching the major shapes and values, prior to painting.

calligraphy actually handwriting, but, in drawing and painting, refers to lines that have the quality of beautiful handwriting (calligraphic lines) and/or brushed lines that are similar to Oriental writing.

caricature a drawing, painting, or sculpture (usually of a person) that exaggerates selected characteristics of the subject (such as a prominent chin or large eyes). Often humorous.

cartoon a drawing (often for publication) that symbolizes or caricatures a person or event. Animated cartoons are drawings that are placed on film to create the illusion of movement.

center of interest the area of a work of art toward which all visual movement is directed. It is the visual focal point of the work.

cityscape a painting or drawing that uses elements of the city (buildings, streets, shops) as subject matter.

collage a technique in which the artist glues materials, such as paper, cloth, or found materials, to some type of background.

collagraph a type of print, made by inking a surface that contains glued materials in low relief.

color an element of design that identifies natural and manufactured things as being red, yellow, blue, orange, etc.

color harmony the use of several colors from the color wheel arrangement that produce certain desirable combinations.

commercial artist a person who works in the area of graphic communications and/or utilitarian or reproductive art forms. A distinction is often made between a commercial artist and a *fine artist*, who produces unique works for their own merit, not for commercial purposes.

communication the methods of letting others know what you are thinking, saying, and feeling. It may be verbal, visual, musical, or physical. Artists are concerned with visual communication.

complementary colors any two colors that are opposite each other on the color wheel. When mixed, they will tend to subdue the intensities and produce a grayed hue.

complex composed of many interconnected parts.

composition the arrangement of the parts in a work of art, usually according to the principles of design.

concept art a style of art in which the artist expresses the idea (concept) of a proposed work of art in verbal or diagram form. The actual work will probably not be carried out.

conceptualized art a style of painting or sculpture in which the artist communicates what is known of the subject (a general idea), not how the subject actually looks. An African tribal mask is a conceptualized face.

construction an additive sculptural technique in which parts are added, assembled, and adhered until the work is finished.

contemporary art refers to the art of today; the methods, styles, and techniques of artists living now.

contrast a principle of design that refers to differences in values, colors, textures, and other elements in an artwork to achieve emphasis and interest.

contour drawing a single line drawing that defines the outer (and sometimes inner) edges of people or objects.

cool colors the hues on one side of the color wheel which contain blues and greens.

craft skill, ingenuity, dexterity.

crafts works of art that generally have a utilitarian purpose (ceramics, macramé, leather work, metals, weaving, fabrics, jewelry, furniture design, and so on).

craftsmanship skill, knowledge and dexterity applied to works of art in any field. Generally refers to skill in producing expertly finished products. Expert workmanship.

craftsperson a person who works in any of the areas of the crafts (ceramics, fabrics, knotting, jewelry, weaving, leather, enamelling, and so on).

Cubism a style of art in which the subject is broken apart and reassembled in an abstract form, emphasizing geometric shapes.

culture refers to elements that add to the esthetic aspects of our lives, enriching them with beauty and enjoyment.

diagonal at an angle, neither vertical nor horizontal.

distort to deform or stretch something out of its normal shape.

doodling an absent-minded type of drawing in which the person is often preoccupied with other thoughts.

dynamic full of energy; in a state of imbalance or tension; constantly changing and active.

earth works works of artists that are excavated in the surface of the earth, usually in desert areas. They are best viewed from above, from a plane or helicopter.

easel painting any kind of painting that is done in a studio (on an easel) and can be transported from place to place. Not painted directly on a wall, such as a mural.

ellipse a curved line that is drawn to produce an oval shape with specific geometric proportions.

elongated stretched out lengthwise; drawn in a way as to exaggerate height or length.

emphasis a principle of design by which the artist or designer may use opposing sizes, shapes, contrasting colors, or other means to place greater attention on certain areas or objects.

engraving the process of incising lines into a surface to create an image.

expressionism any style of art in which the artist tries to communicate strong personal and emotional feelings to the viewers. If written with a capital "E," it refers to a definite style of art, begun in Germany early in the twentieth century.

eye level a horizontally drawn line that is even in height with your eye. In perspective drawing, it can be the actual distant horizon line, but it can also be drawn in a close-up still life.

fashion illustrator a person who draws fashion designs for advertisements in magazines, newspapers, etc.

figure drawing drawing that uses the human figure as its chief subject matter.

fine artist a person who produces artwork that is unique and has a noncommercial function, such as an easel painting, wall sculpture, or serigraph that decorates or enhances a home, office, or public place.

form an element of design that is three-dimensional and encloses volume (cube, sphere, pyramid, cylinder, and free flowing). Similar to *shape*, which encloses area.

fragmented broken or divided into several parts. A fragmented painting may have several separated parts that are arranged to complete the composition.

free form   not having prescribed geometric proportions.

frieze   a decorative band, usually patterned, that decorates a wall.

gallery   a commercial enterprise that exhibits and sells works of art. Sometimes it is used in reference to an art museum.

geometric art   a type of art that uses lines and shapes that recall geometry: triangles, squares, rectangles, arcs, straight lines, circles, and so on.

gesture drawing   a scribbly type of line drawing that catches the movements and gestures of an active figure.

graphic artist   a person who designs packages and advertisements for newspapers and magazines; illustrates for ads, books, and magazines; draws cartoons; designs displays and signs; produces any kind of art for reproduction.

graphics   refers to the art of drawing, and techniques that stress the use of lines and strokes to portray images and ideas.

grid   a pattern developed by crossing vertical and horizontal lines.

ground   the surface on which a drawing, painting, or collage is done, such as paper, canvas, or cardboard.

hard edge   refers to a style of art in which the artist uses crisp, clean edges and applies values or colors so that they are even and flat.

harmony   *see* color harmony

high-keyed   describes colors or values that are light tints and have white mixed with them. Pastel colors are high-keyed.

high relief   a surface that has much variation between the highest and lowest points.

horizon line   an actual or imaginary line that runs across a piece of art, defining the place where sky and earth come together.

hue   the name of a color, such as yellow, yellow-orange, green.

impasto   a thick, heavy application of paint by paintbrush or knife.

Impressionism   a style of drawing and painting begun in France in about 1875. It stresses an off-hand (candid) glimpse of the subject, and an emphasis on the momentary effects of light on color.

industrial design   design of products for consumer or industrial use. An industrial designer might design computer terminals, telephones, light bulbs, staple guns, or locomotives.

intensity   the strength, brightness, or purity of a color. The more intense the color, the less it is weakened with admixtures of neutrals or its complementary color.

interior design   design that emphasizes the esthetic arrangement and decoration of living and working environments, including walls, furniture, and artistic additions.

kinetic art   any three-dimensional sculpture that contains moving parts. Motion can be started either by air currents or some type of motor.

landscape   a work of art that shows the features of the natural environment (trees, lakes, mountains, flowers, and so forth).

layout design   an area of art in which designers are concerned with the arrangement of pictures, type, and lettering on a flat surface.

line   an element of design that may be two-dimensional (pencil on paper), three-dimensional (wire or rope), or implied (the edge of a shape or form).

linear perspective   a system of drawing to give the illusion of depth on a flat surface. All straight, parallel lines receding into the distance are drawn to one or more vanishing points in such a drawing.

logo   a visual design that symbolizes and stands for a company, industry, or individual. It usually (but not always) uses letters, numbers, or some recognizable visual element.

low-keyed   describes colors or values that are dark shades (have black mixed with them).

low relief   a surface that has only slight variations between the highest and lowest parts.

minimal art   a style of painting or sculpture in which the least possible decoration is used. A single flat square on a plain background is an example of minimal art.

mixed media   a two-dimensional art technique that uses more than one medium, for example, a crayon and watercolor drawing.

moiré   a wavelike pattern that develops when certain lines are overlapped. It occurs in some Op Art designs.

monochromatic   of only one color. Most drawings are monochromatic, using one color of ink or lead. If a painting uses only one hue and variations mixed by adding neutrals, it is monochromatic.

motif   the dominant idea or feature in a work of art. Also, the two- or three-dimensional configuration that is repeated in a pattern.

movement   a principle of design that refers to the arrangement of parts in a work of art to create a slow to fast movement of your eye through the work.

museum   a place in the community where art is collected and placed on view. Works belonging to the museum are not for sale, but for study and enjoyment.

negative space   the area around the objects in a drawing or painting. Often called the background.

neutral   in working with color, refers to white, black, and gray, which have no discernable hues.

non-objective art   art that has no recognizable subject matter, such as trees, flowers, or people. The actual subject matter might be color or the composition of the work itself.

Op Art (Optical Art) a style of art (originated in the mid-twentieth century) that uses optical (visual) illusions of many types. These works are composed to confuse, heighten, or expand visual sensations.

opaque the quality of a material that will not let light pass through. The opposite of transparent.

organic free form, or a quality that resembles living things. The opposite of mechanical or geometric.

outline a line drawn around the outer shape of a person or thing (the edge of a silhouette).

oval egg-shaped; a general circular shape that is longer than it is wide.

painterly quality the quality of a work of art that allows brush strokes to show and lets us see that it is really a painting.

pattern a principle of design in which combinations of lines, colors, and shapes are used to show real or imaginary things. Pattern may also be achieved by repeating a shape, line, or color.

persepective drawing a method of drawing on a flat surface (which is two-dimensional) to give the illusion of depth or the third dimension.

picture plane the flat surface which the artist uses as a starting point for his/her work. It is not the paper or canvas itself, but an imaginary flat plane that the artist uses as a visual reference, and which is at the same level or depth as the surface itself.

pigment the coloring material used in making painting and drawing media. Pigments may be natural (from earth, plant dyes, and so on) or from laboratory-prepared chemicals.

Pop Art a twentieth-century style of art that features the everyday, popular things around us. A painting of a large Coke bottle might be considered Pop Art.

portrait a piece of artwork featuring a person, several people, or perhaps an animal. Portraits are usually facial, but they can also show full figures.

positive space the objects in a work of art, as opposed to the background or space around the objects.

Post-Impressionism the style of art that immediately followed the Impressionists, in France. Paul Cézanne was a leader of this style, which stressed more substantial subjects than the Impressionists, and a conscious effort to design the surface of the painting.

printmaker an artist who works in any of the printmaking media, producing multi-original art, such as serigraphs, woodcuts, linoleum cuts, lithographs, etchings, or experimental prints.

proportion a comparative size relationship between several objects or between the parts of a single object or person. In drawing and painting, for example, the correct relationship between the size of head and body.

radial balance a design based on a circle, with features radiating from a central point.

Realism a style of art that attempts to show actual places, people, or objects realistically. It stresses actual colors, textures, shadows, and arrangements.

refraction the change in appearance or the visual distortion that occurs when objects are viewed partly through water, glass, prisms, or other transparent media.

relief the raised parts of a surface that are often noticeable by the feeling of texture. Relief is actually the difference between the highest and lowest parts of a work.

Renaissance a period of time (about A.D. 1400–1600) following the Middle Ages that featured an emphasis on human beings and their environment, on science, and on philosophy. Many of the principles of design were instituted by Renaissance artists.

rendering the careful and complete drawing of an object, place, or person to make it appear realistic.

representational drawing the drawing of objects, people, or places in such a way that they can be recognized for what they are.

rhythm a principle of design that indicates a type of movement in an artwork or design, often by repeated shapes or colors.

rubbings a technique that transfers the textural quality of a surface to paper by placing the paper over the textured surface and rubbing the top of the paper with a crayon, pencil, or other drawing implement.

seascape a work of art that features some part of the sea or coastal environment as subject matter.

set-up a group of objects that are arranged to be drawn or painted. A still life grouping.

sgraffito the process of scratching lines into the surface of a work of art to expose the surface underneath.

shade the darker tone (value) of a hue, made by adding an amount of black to the original hue.

shading using the drawing or painting medium to form darkened areas (shadows) that will help produce a feeling of space depth.

shape an element of design described that is two-dimensional and encloses area. Shape can be divided into two basic classes: *geometric* (square, triangle, circle) and *organic* (irregular in outline).

simulated textures areas that have the appearance of textured surfaces, where no texture actually exists.

sketch a quick drawing that catches the immediate feeling of action or the impression of a place. Probably not a completed drawing, but one that may be a reference for later work.

space an element of design that indicates areas in a drawing (positive and negative) and/or the feeling of depth in a two-dimensional work of art.

spectrum the complete range of color that is present in a band of light (and seen when that light is refracted through a prism). The colors of the rainbow.

static showing no movement or action.

still life an arrangement of inanimate objects to draw or paint.

structure the constructive elements of a work of art; the underlying arrangement of the parts of the composition.

style the distinctive character contained in the works of art of one person, period of time, or geographical location.

stylist an artist whose main concern is the modification and redesign of automobiles.

stylization to conform to a certain style or "look" of art.

subjective space the personal depiction of the quality of space in a work of art in which the artist does not use the conventional means of perspective.

subject matter the subject of a composition; what the artist wants to communicate.

subtle in art, describes the delicate appearance or gradual change contained in the work of art such as in color or value.

Super Realism (Photo Realism) a twentieth-century style of drawing and painting that emphasizes photographic realism. Many times the objects are greatly enlarged yet keep their photographic appearance.

Surrealism a style of twentieth-century painting in which artists relate normally unrelated objects and situations. Often the scenes are dreamlike or set in unnatural surroundings.

symmetrical balance a design in which both sides are identical.

technique any method or system of working with materials.

tension *see* visual tension.

texture an element of design that refers to the surface: whether it is rough, smooth, or soft, for example. It can be actual or simulated (implied).

tint the lighter tone (value) of a hue, made by adding an amount of white to the original hue.

tone the modification of a color (hue) through the addition of neutrals (black, white, or gray).

tooth the textural "feel" of a sheet of paper.

traditional art any style of art that treats the subject matter in a natural (rather realistic) way.

translucent transmitting light in a diffused form, but not allowing objects to be seen clearly. A thin sheet of white paper is translucent.

transparent allowing light to pass through in an unobstructed way, and allowing objects to be seen clearly. A sheet of clear glass is transparent.

triadic color harmony a combination of three hues, equidistant from each other on the color wheel, such as orange, green, and violet.

unity a principle of design that relates to the sense of oneness or wholeness in a work of art.

value an element of design that relates to the lightness and darkness of a color or tone.

vanishing point in perspective drawing, an imaginary point or points on the eye level toward which parallel lines recede and where they will eventually meet.

vertical upright and parallel to the sides of the paper.

visual environment everything that surrounds you. Usually divided into two groupings: the *natural* environment (trees, flowers, water, sky, rocks, and so on) and the *manufactured* or *man-made* environment (buildings, roads, bridges, automobiles, schools, and so on).

visual tension a sense or feeling of visual strain that is produced in an artwork through contrast, imbalance, crowding, stretching, constricting, or similar visual devices. It often adds a feeling of excitement to a work of art.

wash a color of ink or watercolor that is diluted with water to make it lighter in value and more transparent.

white glue any of the poly-vinyl-acetate glues on the market, each having its own trade name.

Index

Acknowledgments

This book is the distillation of many years of teaching experience on the part of the authors and their colleagues. The three primary authors, Joseph Gatto, Albert Porter, and Jack Selleck, have worked with students and student teachers at all levels. Their common concern with excellence of design is the basis for this book. Their diligence, knowledge, and cooperation are exceptional.

Davis Publications and their staff are to be congratulated on their forward-looking policy toward student- and teacher-related art materials, and particularly for undertaking this project in design, something which has been treated lightly in the past.

Many artists and photographers responded to the authors' calls for help in gathering visual materials, and we offer them our sincerest thanks: Ansel Adams, Ralph Bacerra, Will Barnet, Jordi Bonet, Colleen Browning, Dr. Bob Burningham, Robert Caddes, Al Ching, Dorte Christjansen, Richard Diebenkorn, Charles Eames, James Fuller, Jason Hailey, Barkley L. Hendricks, Rick Herold, George Horn, Win Jones, Claude Kent, Jerome Kirk, Gabe Kreisworth, Roger Kuntz, Clint MacKenzie, Sam Maloof, John Muelmeister, Perry Owen, Britt Phillips, Ann Plauzoles, Kiyoshi Saito, Ray Schutte, John and Marion Scott, Kay Sekinachi, Walt Selleck, Don Sevart, Doug Smith, Michael Stone, Wayne Thom, Andy Warhol, Paul Wegeman, Helmut Wielander, Susan Woirol, and Robert E. Wood.

Thanks also to the staffs of museums that share parts of their collections with us in this book: The Albright-Knox Art Gallery, Buffalo, New York; The Art Institute of Chicago; The Baltimore Museum of Art; The Museum of Art, Carnegie-Mellon University; Hirschhorn Museum and Sculpture Garden and the National Collection of Fine Arts, Smithsonian Institute; The Los Angeles County Museum of Art; The Los Angeles Museum of Natural History; The Museum of Contemporary Crafts, New York; The Museum of Modern Art, New York; The National Gallery of Art, Washington, D. C.; The Norton Simon Museum of Art at Pasadena; The Philadelphia Museum of Art; The San Francisco Museum of Modern Art; and the Yale University Art Gallery.

Several galleries, representing contemporary artists, have shared the work of their special people: Leo Castelli Gallery, New York; Corbier and Ekstrom Gallery, New York; Hirschl and Adler Galleries, New York; The Kennedy Galleries, New York; and the Orlando Gallery, Encino, California.

A number of companies, corporations, and associations assisted in providing visual materials for the book: The Automobile Club of Southern California; Baskin Robbins Ice Cream Company; Bethlehem Steel Corporation; British Leyland Motors; Cunningham and Walsh, Inc.; Design Research Corporation; Interpace Tile Inc.; Levi Strauss, Inc.; National Aeronautics and Space Administration; Polaroid Corporation; Saul Bass and Associates; 7-Up Company; and Warner Brothers Records.

The authors' wives are also thanked, for making the time and space available for research and writing. And a heartfelt thanks to George Horn, who offered many helpful ideas in the formulation and finalization of the text.

All of us—authors and contributors—hope the result has been worth the effort, and that design will always have a more meaningful part in your life.

G.F.B.